Digital Rights Management: The Problem of Expanding Ownership Rights

CHRISTOPHER MAY

Chandos Publishing
Oxford · England

Chandos Publishing (Oxford) Limited
Chandos House
5 & 6 Steadys Lane
Stanton Harcourt
Oxford OX29 5RL
UK
Tel: +44 (0) 1865 884447 Fax: +44 (0) 1865 884448
Email: info@chandospublishing.com
www.chandospublishing.com

First published in Great Britain in 2007

ISBN:
978 1 84334 124 6 (paperback)
978 1 84334 185 7 (hardback)
1 84334 124 7 (paperback)
1 84334 185 9 (hardback)

© Christopher May, 2007

Typeset by Domex e-Data Pvt. Ltd.
Printed in Great Britain by Biddles Ltd., King's Lynn, Norfolk

Digital Rights Management: The Problem of Expanding Ownership Rights

CHANDOS
INFORMATION PROFESSIONAL SERIES

Series Editor: Ruth Rikowski
(email: Rikowskigr@aol.com)

Chandos' new series of books are aimed at the busy information professional. They have been specially commissioned to provide the reader with an authoritative view of current thinking. They are designed to provide easy-to-read and (most importantly) practical coverage of topics that are of interest to librarians and other information professionals. If you would like a full listing of current and forthcoming titles, please visit our web site **www.chandospublishing.com** or contact Hannah Grace-Williams on email info@chandospublishing.com or telephone number +44 (0) 1865 884447.

New authors: we are always pleased to receive ideas for new titles; if you would like to write a book for Chandos, please contact Dr Glyn Jones on email gjones@chandospublishing.com or telephone number +44 (0) 1865 884447.

Bulk orders: some organisations buy a number of copies of our books. If you are interested in doing this, we would be pleased to discuss a discount. Please contact Hannah Grace-Williams on email info@chandospublishing.com or telephone number +44 (0) 1865 884447.

For Hilary

Contents

Preface

This book is about the seemingly technical issue of Digital Rights Management (DRM). However, what I will be arguing is that this is a technology that we all need to understand, not least as it has the potential to undermine many information-related freedoms we (as consumers) may feel that we should enjoy. For example, where DRM software uses an internet connection to report back to sellers (rights owners), not only does this have an impact on our privacy, it may also have implications for the security of our computer. In this sense DRM is a good example of the question that has been the centre of my writing on intellectual property for many years: how can we ensure that there is a fair and equitable balance between the legitimate rights of (intellectual) property owners, and the *equally* legitimate rights of consumers and users of knowledge and information?[1]

One recent example of how DRM may have an effect on our lives is amply demonstrated by the disputes surrounding the deployment by Sony/BMG of DRM software on CDs by Van Zant (and other artists). Mark Russinovich, who discovered the hidden software after experiencing some problems with his computer (having played the CD), found that this software allowed Sony to take over an element of his computer and therefore compromise its security. It inserted into his computer's software a 'back door' allowing the company access (without notification or authorisation) to his hard disk and all material stored on it. This software, known as a 'rootkit', also effectively hid itself and was designed to be very difficult to remove, a strategy often adopted by writers of viruses and other 'malware'. After widespread criticism, and initially denying that the DRM-programme was harmful or undermined security of users computers, Sony/BMG issued a patch that left many of the problems in place according to Mr Russinovich, and indeed in some ways made them worse.[2]

Microsoft finally declared Sony's DRM software a security risk after it became obvious that it was not possible to ignore the disruption it caused to Windows, and security companies such as Symantec began alerting PC users to its existence. In itself, this led some to wonder about collusion between Sony/BMG and those companies that claim to provide tools to protect our computers; whose interests are they really protecting – ours, or Sony's? However, following these actions Sony undertook the recall of some 4.7m music CDs, 2.1m of which had already been sold to consumers, with a final legal settlement including a compensation package of either a $7.50 cash payment together with a free album download or three free downloads for each consumer, in addition to a replacement CD.[3]

However, this was not the only issue Sony's 'rootkit' raised: the Electronic Frontier Foundation reported that the Sony/BMG End User Licence Agreement that covers this CD software itself contained a number of elements of concern. Apart from including stringent limitations on the circumstances in which the music files may be retained on an individual's computer, the licence allows Sony/BMG the right to install and use 'backdoors' in the software to 'enforce their rights' without prior notice. And although this gives Sony/BMG access to consumers' computers, as with most, if not all, software, the licence also disclaims any liability for harm or damage their interventions may cause (von Lohman, 2005). Certainly, some might argue that this is an extreme case of how companies might deploy DRM, but none of these actions were illegal. Moreover, DRM can clearly have considerable adverse effects on consumers and other users and producers of content, from commercial buyers of software and other informational products, to universities, libraries and other public repositories of information and knowledge. Perhaps more ominously, this illustrates how intellectual property owners feel that they can ride roughshod over others' rights and interests; Thomas Hesse, Sony BMG's president of global digital business argued that 'Most people don't even know what a rootkit is, so why should they care about it' (quoted in Schneier, 2005). Despite finally being forced to compensate purchasers of the discs which contained the rootkit, and having presented a partial apology, with around half-a-million computers infected with this (albeit) 'legal' spyware, Sony made no undertaking not to include similar software in future products.[4]

Therefore, the rationale for this book is to shine some light on this particular nexus where technology and intellectual property meet, because, as with most things, forewarned is forearmed.

Notes

1. See, for instance, May (2000, 2007) and May and Sell (2005).
2. 'Sony tries to patch up piracy row', BBC News online, 9 November 2005; Naughton (2005).
3. 'Free downloads end Sony CD saga', BBC News online, 23 May 2006.

4. The case is discussed at some length in Schneier (2005), while the details of the final settlement are laid out in 'Legal Fallout from Sony's CD Woes', BBC News online, 3 January 2006 and 'Free downloads end Sony CD saga', BBC News online, 23 May 2006.

Acknowledgements

Any writer needs to acknowledge many debts both direct and indirect when completing a book. This project has benefited greatly from the analysis of DRM that I developed in my work with Jill Johnstone of the National Consumer Council, and I would like to thank her for encouraging me to think about these issues for the NCC. As with all my work on intellectual property and related issues, I owe a massive debt of gratitude to Professor Susan Sell with whom I have been working for some years, not least on our recently published critical history of intellectual property rights (IPRs). Over the last couple of years a number of other people have also aided the development of my analysis of DRM, and I will take the chance to thank them here (with apologies if there is anyone who I have inadvertently missed): Patricia Akester, Andrew Chadwick, Marianne Franklin, Vera Franz, Brian Lloyd, Duncan Matthews and Geoff Tansey.

In the final stages of finishing of the manuscript, Adrian Geisow and Graeme Hughes both very kindly read the entire manuscript, and their comments, criticisms and suggestions have helped me clarify and refine the argument. Finally, I would like to thank Glyn Jones and the team at Chandos, who encouraged me to expand and develop this analysis from an article that originally appeared on-line in *First Monday*. Their enthusiasm for this project, and patience with me when I had to delay delivery of the manuscript due to moving institutions and taking on expanded professional responsibilities, was a great help. Finally, I could not continue to work without the love and support of my wife, Hilary Jagger, and as always it is to her that I dedicate this book.

About the author

Christopher May is Professor of Political Economy and Head of the Department of Politics and International Relations, Lancaster University UK. He is series co-editor (with Nicola Phillips) of the *International Political Economy Yearbook*, and edited volume 15 of *Global Corporate Power* (Lynne Rienner, 2006). He has been widely published on the subjects of intellectual property rights and the information society. His work has been translated into Arabic, Chinese, French, German, Swedish and Ukrainian. With Susan Sell, he co-authored *Intellectual Property Rights: A Critical History* (Lynne Rienner, 2005), and more recently wrote the first independent book-length study of the *World Intellectual Property Organisation* (Routledge, 2006). His current research focuses on the impact of 'openness' on the global political economy, and he is also interested in the 'rule of law' in the new millennium. Before becoming an academic he has worked in the music industry, as a bookseller, and for the political pressure group Charter 88.

Introduction:
setting the scene

This book is concerned with a set of technologies that have only been widely deployed in the last decade: digital rights management (DRM) tools. However, while other books may set out the technical issues and problems of deploying DRM to protect a companies' knowledge or informational 'assets', this book is concerned with the political economy of DRM. If you are looking for a manual on how to implement a DRM system for your company, or conversely if you are seeking advice on how to circumnavigate the constrictions such programmes put on use, this book is going to be little help. Rather, the purpose of this book is to examine the role and function that DRM plays in the contemporary 'information society' and to explore the problems and issues, specifically related to intellectual property, that the deployment of these technologies raises. Moreover, recognising the political economic context in which DRM has been deployed, this book also examines (albeit relatively briefly) the response that the use of DRM has provoked in the markets where it has been most evident.

While in the past these technologies were often referred to as 'copy-protection' systems, the content industries have shifted to the terminology of DRM as it is likely to have fewer negative connotations, although the term Technical Protection Measures is also sometimes used in discussions of these types of software. Given the widespread use of the term Digital Rights Management by both supporters and critics, I have deployed it throughout this book – although this should not be taken as accepting its relatively neutral resonance (no-one who finishes reading this book will think I am neutral about DRM). Certainly, it might be more accurate to refer to 'content control' technology or perhaps even 'Digital Rights Restrictions' but neither of these terms is in common use.[1]

This book focuses on the crucial relationship between intellectual property rights (IPRs) and social norms of information and/or knowledge use to highlight the disturbance, or even challenge, that DRM represents to previous legitimated practices in the regulation of the commodification of knowledge and information. To do this, in the next chapter I set out the relationship between the protection of IPRs and the new models of business that have been developed in the 'information age' (i.e. digital distribution, and e-commerce). A number of problems have arisen as regards the ownership and (re)use of digital content, and here these are directly related to past and present social norms of consumption. Therefore, I focus on the central issue of the continuing political controversies regarding the balance between private rights to reward and public goods of information dissemination and use. I also relate elements of the history of this balance to specific aspects of technological development (such as the advent of video recorders). Thus, by setting DRM in the context of the politics of IPRs I begin to develop the argument about the damage that the employment of DRM does to the previous social bargains by which users' and owners' interests have historically been balanced.

This then leads me, in Chapter three, to examine the two main directions in which DRM has been developed to deal with the problems identified in the previous chapter.

These I call 'hard' DRM and 'soft' DRM to distinguish their logic as regards the central relationship between user and owner. I set out each form's character and method of rights' protection, while also noting that, while this is a clean analytical distinction, in the real world of DRM there are often hybrid approaches with much less of a clear-cut distinction between these two 'logics'. Thus, I examine the advantages each trajectory represents for users (or rights' holders), as well as the general problems each approach represents for the balance between private rights and public goods. This chapter develops a general analytical context for the case studies presented in the next chapter.

In Chapter four I take the more general issues developed in the previous two chapters and apply them to two cases, both of which have become paradigmatic of the issues that surround DRM:

The music industry. In this sub-section, I explore the manner in which DRM has been presented as the answer to a set of Internet related 'problems' identified by commentators both within and outside the recorded music business. These issues are directly related to similar issues as regards previous (re)recording technologies, and as such this has led to a certain level of scepticism as regards this proposed solution to 'piracy'. Returning to the issues of social norms of consumption, as well as wider market issues, I conclude that the 'solution' of DRM may misunderstand the problem. This case study has, of course, a wider significance due to the emblematic place the music industry holds as regards other content industries.

The software industry. In this sub-section, I explore the manner in which DRM tools have already been extensively deployed in the realm of software to deal with the problems of unauthorised copying and distribution of software packages. In software, however, in many ways the move to stringent DRM has encouraged the further expansion of the Free and Open Source Software (FOSS) movement. Thus, the deployment of DRM in software has prompted not only complaint and critique (as it has in the music industry) but also direct 'resistance' through the breaking of DRM protections and the illegal use of software. Perhaps, more importantly, resistance to this model of control has also prompted the adoption of another way of treating creativity on-line. While the FOSS movement is not the central concern of this book, nevertheless I take a little space to explore this particular strategy for avoiding the limitations on use that are established by DRM.

I then draw together the themes of these two case studies to summarise the argument that relates the deployment of DRM to the development of alternatives to this model of control.

In the concluding chapter, I argue that the utilisation of DRM does not, as its supporters suggest, merely return the protection of IPRs to what it was in the past, but rather radically extends and strengthens the rights of owners. This suggests that the solution is considerably worse than the problem it has been developed to address. Therefore, I conclude that DRM is a political issue that needs to be carefully considered by policy makers, information specialists and consumer organisations, and it is not (as is sometimes presented) merely a technical problem simply requiring better regulation. Although the 'information age' may have introduced new methods for the dissemination and use of information and knowledge, this does not mean that previous considerations of the manner in which private rights should be *balanced* with public ones regarding issues of use and access can now be ignored.

However, before working through these arguments, I want to briefly examine the claim that we have become a global information society, encompassing a 'new' information economy, as this is the backdrop for many supporters of the widespread deployment of DRM in global markets for information and knowledge.

A new economy?

Although in many ways in the years since my book *The Information Society: a sceptical view* (May, 2002) appeared much has changed in the domain of information and communications technologies (ICTs), much has also remained remarkably similar. Rather than reprise the whole argument of that book, here I will merely revisit (in general terms) the criticisms that I made of claims that we now work and live in an 'information economy'. My general argument is that IPRs are the legal form of this new (so-called) information age's market relations, and therefore are the form in which the economics of the information society are expressed; they define the 'who owns what' of the 'new economy'. The recognition and legitimisation of IPRs has allowed corporations to consolidate and expand their control of the socio-economic relations of information and knowledge across the emerging global society.[2]

In *The Information Society: a sceptical view*, I identified four linked claims (one overarching claim and three connected more specific claims) in the literature that has proclaimed the arrival (or at least imminent arrival) of the (global) information society: these are:

- that we are experiencing a social revolution;
- that the organisation of economic relations has been transformed;

- that political practices and the communities involved are changing; and
- that the state and its authority are in terminal decline.

Each of these claims is, at the very least, severely overstated in much of the literature that celebrates the establishment of an information society. However, one thing that the 'dotcom' boom and bust achieved was to remove some of the hyperbole from these debates, and therefore since first publishing these views mainstream discussion of the 'information revolution' has to a considerable extent modified the more outlandish expressions of these general arguments. Conversely, it is also necessary to note that the valuations of certain information economy corporations (of which Google is probably the best example) still represent an extraordinary premium over their likely yearly earnings or assets held, reflecting a continuing belief in the transformative potential of ICTs. These four themes still flow through the commentary and media coverage of new ICTs, and therefore to set the context for the discussion of DRM we should (however briefly) engage with the general claim and the specific argument about the 'new economy' (while leaving aside the claim about changes in political practice and the efficacy of the state in a globalised information society).

The 'information age'

At the end of the twentieth century there was a relatively widespread assumption among social commentators and analysts that we were entering a 'new age', prompted by what was often presented as the 'information revolution'. From Nicholas Negroponte at the *MediaLab* telling us in the mid-1990s that the future would involve us all 'being digital', to writers based in London (prominently Diane

Coyle of the *Economist* and Danny Quah at the London School of Economics) asserting that such was the power and importance of information and knowledge that we now lived in a 'weightless world'. On one hand, such claims were dealt a blow when the rise in energy (and specifically, oil) prices in the last few years led to widespread concerns about the impact on the global economy; on the other, the current (at least) lack of a worldwide recession prompted by a rising oil price that would mimic events of the 1970s does suggest that perhaps the notion of weightlessness captures something important about the contemporary global system. Looking at other developments, Manuel Castells assembled a three-volume analysis of what he preferred to call the 'network society'. Whatever else we can say about the veracity or otherwise of various elements of these analyses, and many others, it is plain that they intended to convince us of a social transformation that was taking place, initiated and indeed carried forward through the deployment and use of the new ICTs, focusing predominantly, but not exclusively, on the Internet.

This immediately leads us to recognise a clear problem with much of this literature; there is a tendency to lapse into a casual technological determinism. Indeed, even Castells' monumental three-volume study (now revised) fails to completely side-step this problem. When we ask 'how do we characterise society?', certainly we may want to include some specific technological characteristics of social relations, but can this be the primary determinant of society's character? Arguments about an information society tend to answer 'yes' with the often-unacknowledged (but profound) influence of Alvin Toffler's synthetic meta-history (set out most eloquently in *The Third Wave*) clearly evident. Thus, it has become common to present the new age as following two previous socio-technological 'waves' – the agricultural and the industrial – with a third wave, the informational. Tofler's analysis, drawing on the work of Schumpeter and Kondratiev, is seldom cited or even mentioned in passing in much of the 'information revolution' literature, but the notion of the third wave is almost universally adopted in one form or another.

There are two significant problems with this sort of technological determinism: firstly, the notion that somehow technologies produce social change wrenches such technological changes out of their social context and assumes some level of autonomy for technological developments. This denies the significant political economic underpinnings of any particular technological change, but also suggests that such changes are outside the control of the societies in which they appear: technological change is inevitable, and cannot, indeed *should* not be resisted! Certainly this may serve the purposes of those who wish to propose that certain technological trajectories have no alternative (often the 'owners' of these technologies and/or their allies in the media and academia), but this does not reveal, nor understand, the contested and contingent character of new and modified technologies. Technological change is not only path-dependent, it is firmly located within the political economic and social structures that effect and shape choices about which innovations will be supported, or even proposed, and those which will be ignored, down-played or, in extreme cases, rendered illegal. Crucially, as I will argue later, the emergence of DRM is a direct response to political economic pressures, and not linked to any supposed organic (or 'natural') developmental dynamic for software or technology more widely conceived.

Secondly, and specifically with claims regarding ICTs' ability to transform society, we need to ask which technologies should be regarded as transformative. If we look at the long history of new ICTs, from social technologies such as language and writing, to organisational technologies such as the postal service, through to more mechanical changes, perhaps most obviously Victorian telegraphy, then we can detect in the last twenty years a dangerous fixation with recent developments, i.e. digitising ICTs. If we want to suggest that a social revolution is being caused by technological change around information distribution, then we need to be clear why it is *this* change in communication and information management that will transform society and not some previous stage of the development of ICTs. Of course, more subtle analyses of the information age have started to suggest that these earlier technologies did transform, or modify, society; however, this then, again, leads us away from the novelty of recent developments. If we distinguish between quantitative and qualitative change, it is not necessarily obvious that the newest ICTs offer anything more than a quantitative shift in the realms in which they are deployed. Certainly, we might want to suggest that the quantitative acceleration of information handling and communication has made viable activities that were too expensive or time-consuming in the past, but it is unclear that this shift can be self-evidently identified as a social transformation or revolution in advance (as much of the information society literature attempts to establish). Looking back, we may be able to argue that the introduction of a certain technology was revolutionary, but this is really only possible in hindsight and currently we do not, at least in my view, seem to have reached a point when we can search recent history for such a pivotal social moment.

If we accept that the defining characteristic of contemporary society, in relation to the long history of human development, is that its political economic relations are broadly shaped by capitalism (although in specific countries the 'logic' of capitalism may play out quite differently), then the claim that there has been a social revolution rings particularly hollow. Rather, what we seem to have had in the last quarter of a century (the years of the information revolution) is not merely the continuity of capitalist society but rather the intensification of capitalism. If we take Marx's key characteristics of modern capitalism – constant technological change; velocity of circulation linked to profitability; property relations and commodification; the continued development and extension of the division of labour – what we see is that ICTs have contributed to the expansion and intensification of these aspects of society, not their supercedence.[3]

The 'new economy' and information work

The question of the information revolution's relationship with the social relations of contemporary capitalism brings us to the other claim that is often utilised when the need to deploy DRM is asserted; that alongside the more general argument that the availability of powerful ICTs has prompted a social transformation, we now find ourselves in a 'new economy' – one where intellectual property is more valuable, but also more vulnerable. In the more management-related literature of the late-1990s in particular, there was a constant refrain that this 'new economy' would transform business; while now, perhaps, it is a little quieter, it can still be heard. However, although this claim was dealt a severe blow by the 'dotcom' collapse, its underlying theme of changes in the manner in which economies function (most often directly expressed as changes in work practices) remains significant in discussions of how various countries have become, or are becoming more focused on services, and therefore 'post-industrial'. Moreover, this set of claims has been used to argue that business models and practices must be remade for this 'new economy'.

We are often told that rich counties have seen their service sectors expand relative to manufacturing. However, despite the claims about deterritorialisation as a significant effect of the development of the Internet, this is often focused on domestic economic activity. Certainly, in particular countries domestic activity may be increasingly service related, but this forgets two important aspects of these economic activities. Firstly, services themselves are most often directly related to the (international) trade in manufactured goods – these activities are still concerned with the manufacturing sector's needs or requirements; and, secondly, although manufacturing now often takes place in countries with lower labour costs, this merely means that the activity is taking place elsewhere, *not* that it no longer takes place at all, nor that it is no longer controlled by the home countries' corporations. Thus, if we replace a national myopia with a global view: while there are shifts and changes in the social and technical divisions of labour, these do not in any meaningful way transform the totality of activities undertaken in contemporary human society.

This leads me to the widespread claims regarding the transformation in the world of work, sometimes typified as the rise of the 'creatives', or the rise of new forms of knowledge work. Firstly, the notion that this move to information-related work is a major shift is often presented as if all previous work had been of a Dickensian character; an exaggerated view of the physicality and desperation of industrial work is contrasted with an idealised and unrealistic view of the new sunny world of information work. But when we actually look at the sort of information-related jobs that have emerged, what we see is something a little different. In the new information workplace (typified by the call centre), we encounter significant surveillance (raising issues of worker privacy), intensification of work, and the control of work processes under the patina of empowerment; scripts, narrow answer fields and targets for work-load clearance all reduce levels of worker autonomy. Furthermore, the supposed advantages of moves to project-based working for all except the most in-demand specialists often have a significant similarity to nineteenth-century contracting and piecework, denying and undermining many of the workplace compromises that were wrung from employers through collective action in the last 150 years. Likewise, outsourcing can be seen as a strategy for 'distancing', allowing the core employer to avoid responsibility, and again this is more a move back to the nineteenth century than any *new* form of economic organisation.

When we ask 'what exactly *is* knowledge work?', we encounter a problem in statistical measurement: taken to its logical conclusion, a wide definition suggests that all work involves an element of information or knowledge manipulation (even unskilled work is carried on by sentient, cognitive individuals who have to think – in however rudimentary a way – about what they are doing). This approach makes it difficult to differentiate the 'new' age of information society's work from preceding labour practices; indeed, perhaps typing (the key method of interacting with a computer) is manual work. Thus, a narrow definition of information work is often preferred, using such terms as Robert Reich's 'symbolic analysts', but then we find relatively few work in this way, undermining the claim for social transformation. Thus, frequently, a sleight-of-hand is undertaken: information work is defined narrowly and then for statistical measurement is identified with the service sector overall. This allows for the suggestion that the information sector is expanding swiftly.

Without dwelling at length on the obvious shortcoming of this argument, firstly it is far from clear that all service work is knowledge work (do cleaners, gardeners, hairdressers and gym instructors really meaningfully belong to the new information professions?). Secondly, many tasks that are claimed as new information or knowledge-related services are hardly new jobs in any case, rather they have emerged as separate sectors due to the fragmentation of the division of labour, with corporations focusing on their 'core competencies' and outsourcing activities that used to be carried out in-house. Statistically this may produce a reduction in workers employed by manufacturing companies and an expansion in the numbers employed by service companies (therefore leading to a shift in employment statistics) but this has much less direct impact on the overall numbers conducting each set of tasks.

Finally, and most importantly for the political economy of DRM technologies, there has been a very obvious continuance of property relations linked to the control of the means of production. If knowledge and information are emerging as the most important commercial/economic resources in this 'new economy', as many have suggested, then what is also obvious is that there has been a significant move in the global arena, through the Trade Related Aspects of Intellectual Property Rights (TRIPs) agreement at the World Trade Organisation, to expand and underpin the protection of intellectual property. Rather than indicating, as commentators such as John Perry Barlow and others used to proclaim, that 'information want to be free', the dominant legal form of the 'new economy' demonstrates the well-organised forces of capitalism ensuring that key resources are commodified and owned (for exploitation) by the large-scale corporations who also own and deploy many other forms of property in the global market.

Despite the claims about political economic transformation, what we can actually see is the continuance of work relations that have been established over the last two centuries (with some moves to undermine the compromises that labour and unionisation has managed to wring from the employers), alongside a continued process of commodification (the rendering of economic resources and assets as property), again, reflecting the *normal* processes of capitalism. Certainly, the forms of economic relations may have been changing in some ways, but their underlying character remains as it has been for much of the last two centuries, again suggesting that the claim for a 'new economy' obscures more than it reveals. Thus, the use of DRM tools is merely the latest step by owners to secure and maintain control of valuable economic resources (an analysis that I will develop at length in subsequent chapters). In this sense I also disagree with commentators who regard the arrival of what has been referred to as the 'Age of Access' as prompting a transformation in the logic of the content industries (Lucchi, 2005: 1130–2; Rifkin, 2000). Certainly, the shift to leasing from transfer of ownership may change the business models of various sectors, and indeed may have been made more plausible through the use of DRM, but the underlying relationship between owner and consumer remains one that is defined by, and structured by, the deployment of (intellectual) property rights.

To sum up my sceptical argument, and to present it in a simplified form: while there have been significant shifts and changes in the forms that social activities take, this is by no means the same as suggesting the character, or substance, of society has actually been transformed by the so-called 'information revolution'.[4] Thus, rather than a new society, we remain in an essentially modern capitalist society where there is 'business as usual'. This idea of continuity allows us to understand much more easily the political economy of digital rights management. However, as I will also explore later in this book, a key shift *has* been facilitated by new ICTs *within* the broad contours of contemporary capitalist social organisation; the increasing use of 'open' methods may actually be undermining these attempts to continue commodification of knowledge through the use of DRM tools.[5]

Before moving on to the central arguments of this book, experience suggests that it is useful to clarify exactly what intellectual property is, and also briefly to set out the globalised legal regime that covers intellectual property in computer software.

A brief primer on intellectual property rights: forms and functions

This section briefly sets out some of the basic issues around intellectual property for readers who are relatively new to the subject, and who may not be sure exactly what its various forms entail. This section can be freely skipped by those who already are familiar with the characteristics, purposes and justifications entailed in making knowledge and information property.

What is intellectual property?

When knowledge becomes subject to ownership, intellectual property rights (IPRs) express ownership's legal benefits – most importantly, the ability to charge rent for use, to receive compensation for loss, and payment for transfer. Intellectual property rights are sub-divided into a number of groups, of which two generate the most discussion: industrial intellectual property (patents) and literary or artistic intellectual property (copyrights). Conventionally, the difference between patents and copyrights is presented as between a patent's protection of an idea, and copyright's protection of the expression of an idea, and although increasingly this simple distinction has become difficult to draw for a number of reasons, it remains useful as a starting point. Within the laws of intellectual property, the balance between private rewards and the public interest in relatively free access has been most often expressed through time limits on IPRs, which is to say unlike material property, IPRs are formally temporary. Once their time has expired they enter the public realm of freely-available knowledge.

For patents, the knowledge which is to be registered and thus made property should be applicable in industry. To be patentable an idea must be:

- *new*: not already in the public domain or the subject of a previous patent;

- *non obvious*: it should not be common sense to any accomplished practitioner in the field who having been asked to solve a particular practical problem would see this solution immediately. This is to say, it should not be self-evident using available skills or technologies; and

- *useful*, or *applicable in industry*: it must have a stated function, and could immediately be produced to fulfil this function.

Following enaction of the TRIPs agreement, if these three conditions are fulfilled then an idea can be patented in any of the member countries of the World Trade Organisation. The patent is lodged at the national patent office (or with the European Patent Office), which for an agreed fee will allow others access to the patented knowledge as expressed in the patent document, but perhaps more importantly the office will police and facilitate the punishment of unauthorised usage; patents are an institutionalised bargain between the state and the inventor. The state agrees to ensure the inventor is paid for their idea when others use it (for the term of the patent), and the inventor allows the state to lodge the idea in its public records.

Unlike patent, copyright is concerned with the form of knowledge and information that would normally be termed, 'literary and artistic works'. This is usually expressed in words, symbols, music, pictures, three-dimensional objects, or some combination of these different forms. Copyright therefore covers: literary works (fiction and non-fiction), musical works (of all sorts), artistic works (of two *and* three dimensional form and, importantly, irrespective of content – from 'pure art' and advertising to amateur drawings and your child's doodles), maps, technical drawings, photography, audio-visual works (including cinematic works, video and forms of multi-media), and audio recordings. In some jurisdictions this may stretch to broadcasts and also typographical arrangements of publications. However, the underlying ideas, the plot, the conjunction of colours does not receive protection, only the specific expression attracts copyright.

Copyright is meant to ensure that what is protected should not be reproduced without the express permission of the creator (or the owner of the copyright, which may have been legally transferred to another party by the creator). This is often limited to an economic right, where the creator (or copyright owner) is legally entitled to a share of any return that is earned by the utilisation or reproduction of the copyrighted item. In some jurisdictions, however (principally in continental Europe, and those jurisdictions influenced by the civil law tradition), there is an additional moral right not to have work tampered with or misrepresented. In all cases, failure to agree terms prior to the act of reproduction or duplication may result in any resulting income being awarded to the original copyright holder by the court if an infringement is deemed to have taken place. Unlike patents, however, copyright resides in the work from the moment of creation; all that is required is that the creator can prove that any supposed infringement is a reproduction of the original work, in terms of content, and that it was the product of an intended action of copying.

Especially importantly for the discussion in this book, over the long history of the protection of copyright an idea of 'fair use' (or in Europe, 'fair dealing') has been developed both by courts and by policy-makers. This idea has been used to establish either explicitly or more pragmatically (through case law) the allowance for purchasers of copyrighted work to copy segments for re-use, scholarship and criticism, as well as certain other carefully designated (academic) uses. The key aspect of fair use has been that the continuance of creativity often depends on the reuse or adaptation of segments of already existing (and protected) works, and as copyright is intended to support and maintain creativity, where the protection of rights might constrain such creativity, it should be limited; wholesale copying for re-use (plagiarism) remains an offence even under this relaxation of any claimed absolute copyright. The actual extent of these allowances for fair use, and whether they are actually user *rights* has become a major issue of argument as copyrights have become more valuable to owners, and as DRM has expanded the possibility of control by these owners.

Trademarks, which serve to distinguish the products of one company from another, can be made up of one or more distinctive words, letters, numbers, drawings or pictures, emblems or other graphic representations. Generally, trademarks need to be registered, and in the act of registration a check is carried out to ensure that there are no other companies currently registering the same word, symbol or other representation as a trademark in the sector of the economy nominated by registering company. A history of use of a trademark may establish its viability and support its subsequent legal recognition. Thus, a particular trademark is unlikely to succeed in being registered if it is too similar to, or liable to cause confusion with, a trademark already registered by another company (referred to as 'passing off'). Neither will it attract protection if the term or symbol is already in common use. In some jurisdictions the outward manifestation of packaging, provided that it is not a form necessarily dictated by function, may also be subject to trademark status (of which the most famous case is the Coca Cola bottle).

There are other sorts of intellectual property, from process patents (which are like patents but cover processes as opposed to actual machines) to geographical indicators (such as 'champagne'), but these share the key characteristics noted above; they code a form of information or knowledge as ownable property. However, in the case of geographical indicators this is more like a collective trademark; the indicator is limited in use to a defined group using a specified process (traditional to, or identified with, a specific locale). No-one 'owns' a geographical indicator as such, but those that benefit from its recognition can seek protection from those outside the area trying to 'pass off' their products as the same as those produced in the area. For instance, recent disputes have involved the processes that make ham 'Parma ham', and what exactly makes a 'Melton Mowbray' pork pie distinctive. Geographical indicators, as the above suggest, are often (although not exclusively) concerned with food and drink markets.

It is sometimes also useful to think of trade secrets as intellectual property. Although a form which is not made public, trade secrets allow the control or ownership of knowledge. In one way, the trade secret is the ultimate private knowledge property. However, while in some celebrated cases a trade secret is relied on to maintain a competitive advantage (and again the example of Coca Cola is apposite, along with Kentucky Fried Chicken's 'secret blend of 11 herbs and spices'), in the main those who rely on knowledge as a resource adopt an intellectual property approach to protection, rather than keeping such knowledge completely secret. Indeed, for the knowledge industries it would be counter-productive, impossible even, to function on the basis of knowledge being secret, given the importance of reproduction and transfer of that knowledge to generate income and profit. Intellectual property constructs a balance between public availability and private benefit that allows wider access to knowledge and information than trade secrecy. But, this availability is only within specific legal limits constructed by intellectual property.

Why is intellectual property needed?

Most importantly, while they remain active (that is, while they are within their time limits), IPRs formally construct scarcity of use where none necessarily exists. Knowledge and information, unlike material things, are not necessarily rivalrous; co-incident usage seldom detracts from utility. Most of the time knowledge (before it is made property) does not exhibit the characteristics of material things. Take the example of a hammer as material property: if I own a hammer and we would both like to use it, our utility is compromised by sharing use. I cannot use the hammer while you are, you cannot use it while I am, therefore our intended use is rival. Thus, for you to also use my hammer either you have to accept a compromised utility, relying on my goodwill to allow you to use it when I am not, or you must buy another hammer. The hammer is scarce. However, the *idea* of building something with a hammer and nails is not scarce. If I instruct you in the art of simple construction, once that knowledge has been imparted your use of that information has no effect on my own ability to use the knowledge at the same time; there is no compromise to my utility. We may be fighting over whose turn it is to use the hammer, but we do not have to argue over whose turn it is to use the idea of hammering a nail into a joint – our use of the idea of wood construction is non-rival. Ideas, knowledge and information are generally non-rivalrous.

To be sure, if you and I were both cabinet makers, then instructing you in cabinet construction might lead you to compete for my customers, possibly reducing my income. We might also say that any secrecy regarding my skills was anti-competitive. There are also other cases where knowledge may produce advantages for the holder (called information asymmetries) by enabling a better price to be extracted, or by allowing a market advantage to be gained. Here information and knowledge *is* rivalrous, and wider availability of this knowledge would cause market advantage to be compromised. However, rivalrousness is not necessarily of any wider social benefit: competition is often beneficial to customers, while information asymmetries produce market choices that are not fully informed and which therefore can be harmful.

When information is 'naturally' rivalrous, the social good may be best served by ensuring that it is shared and not hoarded. For instance, many problems for buyers in the second-hand car market could be ameliorated if car dealers where required to reveal *all* they knew about the cars they were selling. This would likely reduce the price they could obtain for much of their stock, but would enhance the general satisfaction (and even safety) of second-hand car buyers. Conversely, if trademarks offer useful information regarding the origin, reputation and quality of goods and services, then allowing anyone to use specific marks reduces their social utility. Here, the imposed scarcity *does* serve a wider social purpose, while also benefiting the owner of the mark who can treat it as a commercial asset (well-known trademarks are often accorded significant monetary value by companies and their shareholders).

To sum up: it is difficult to extract a price for the use of non-rival (knowledge) goods, so a legal form of scarcity (IPRs) is introduced to ensure a price can be obtained for use. Where use does not reveal the information content of the product, trade secrecy may be used (and as noted above, recipes are the obvious example), but these circumstances are quite limited. Where revealing information is required legal protection (as with patent registration) is needed, but the law does not construct a scarcity of knowledge itself but the scarcity (limitation) on *use* of such knowledge in commercial activities.

This is because material property is 'naturally' scarce and therefore already is rival in potential use, whereas knowledge in most cases is non-rival prior to becoming intellectual property, and thus can be used by many people at the same time with no necessary conflict between them. Therefore, as Arnold Plant stressed seventy years ago, unlike 'real' property rights, patents (and other IPRs):

> ... are not a *consequence* of scarcity. They are the deliberate creation of statute law; and, whereas in general the institution of private property makes for the preservation of scarce goods, tending (as we might somewhat loosely say) to lead us "to make the most of

them", property rights in patents and copyright make possible the *creation* of scarcity of the products appropriated which could not otherwise be maintained. Whereas we might expect the public action concerning private property would normally be directed at the prevention of the raising of prices, in these cases the object of the legislation is to confer the power of raising prices by enabling the creation of scarcity. (Plant, 1934: 31)

The protection of rights for the express purpose of raising prices is, of course, the central issue that the politics of intellectual property has to deal with. This means that significant political effort has been put in over the years to justify and legitimate the making of property from knowledge and information.

How is property in knowledge usually justified?

In contemporary debates the assertion that there is a clear metaphorical link, indeed a workable similarity, between property in material objects and property in knowledge, information or intellectual creations, is promoted as unproblematic. Here, I will summarise the three main narratives used to justify intellectual property based on this metaphorical relationship which I have explored at greater length elsewhere (May, 2000: Chapter one). Not only commentators but also legal documents and judgements, sometimes explicitly, but more often implicitly, draw on these material property-related narratives to justify the recognition of property in knowledge. These justifications are also used in the TRIPs agreement and have been mobilised in cases brought to the WTO's dispute settlement mechanism. Therefore, they play a profound and important role in the way the global regime of protection of IPRs is governed (and developed through legal precedent).

The first narrative argues for labour's dessert: the effort that is put into the improvement of nature requires that it should be rewarded. In John Locke's influential formulation this was modelled on the improvement of land (Locke, 1690 [1988]). The application of effort to produce crops and/or improved resource yields justified the ownership of specific tracts of land by whoever worked to produce such improvement. Starting from this initial position Locke then argued there was also a right in disposal, mediated by money. This led him to conclude that all property, even after its initial sale or transfer, could be justified on the basis it had originally been produced through the labour of an individual. More importantly, property was also justified because it encouraged the improvement of nature through the reward of effort. Therefore the Lockean argument supports property by suggesting property encourages individual effort through the reward of ownership of the fruits of work. In contemporary debates around intellectual property, the argument that patents and other intellectual properties reward the effort that has been put into their development (the research investment made to develop a patented innovation; the marketing expense in establishing a trademark) has become commonplace.

However, sometimes this argument is supported through the mobilisation of another, secondary story; the notion of property's links with the self as originally proposed by Georg Hegel (Hegel, 1821 [1967]). If we recognise ourselves through the things we own and use – that is, our social existence is directly related to our things – then for Hegel the control and ownership of property is a significant part of the (re)production of selfhood. It is the manner in which individuals protect themselves from the invasions and attacks of others. For Hegel, the state legislates for property as part of its bargain with civil society. Individuals allow the state to operate in certain areas, but protect their individuality (and sovereignty) through the limitations that property rights put upon the state vis-à-vis the individual's own life and possessions. In intellectual property law on the European continent this supports the inalienable moral rights that creators retain over their copyrights even after their formal transfer to new owners. In Anglo-Saxon law this narrative has been less often used due to its implications for the final alienability of intellectual property. Nonetheless, especially where 'passing off' of trademarks (the unauthorised use of logos and brand names, often on substandard goods), and the pirating of copyrighted material (sampling of music, for instance) are concerned, this narrative of justification can sometimes be noted in the calls for redress based on the diminution of reputation, or the ownership of (self) expression.

There is a third narrative of justification which additionally often underpins the role of intellectual property. In this pragmatic or economic argument, the emergence of property rights are presented as a response to the needs of individuals wishing to allocate resources among themselves. Thus, Douglas North argues that in any society the enjoyment of benefits (and the allocation of costs) related to activity takes place through the use and exchange of useful resources. The institution of property arose to ensure that such resources have attached to them the benefits (and the costs) that accrue to their use, and this increases 'efficiency' (North, 1990: pp. 34–5). In this story, property rights took the place of social (trust) relations, and allowed complex trade relations to form over distance.

Mobilising one possible history of material property, this third story suggests that efficient resource use is established through the use of markets in which property is exchanged and transferred to those who can make best use of it. The development of modern economies is predicated therefore on the institution of property, and its ability to ensure the efficient use of limited resources. In this justification, it is this efficiency requirement that drives the historical development of property rights, and now underpins the commodifcation of knowledge. This (institutionalist) retelling of the history of property carries with it the notion that property arose to ensure the efficient allocation of scarce economic resources. Even when it is accepted that this allocation may not be 'optimal', property rights are still presented as the most efficient method of allocation available even though they often produce a less than perfect solution. In the interests of 'efficiency', property as an institution is reproduced (and 'improved') through its legal and social use. This narrative of the efficient allocation of scarce resources is then bought to bear on the allocation and use of knowledge by any number of industries and corporations.

As a subset of this third justification (but linked to the first), one of the most common arguments explicitly utilised to substantiate IPRs is the need to support innovation. Drawing from Locke the notion of reward for effort in improvement, and from the third narrative the idea of social efficiency, it is often asserted that without IPRs there would be little stimulus for innovation. Why would anyone work towards a new invention, a new solution to a problem, if they were unable to profit from its social deployment? Thus, not only does intellectual property reward intellectual effort, it actually stimulates activities that have a social value, and therefore serves to support the social good of progress. Underlying this argument is a clear perception of what drives human endeavour: individual benefit. Only by encouraging and rewarding the individual creator or inventor (with property, and therefore market-related benefits), can any society ensure that it will continue to develop important and socially valuable innovations, which will serve to make society as a whole more efficient.

These arguments or stories are often deployed subtly and in varying combinations, but the key issue is that because intellectual property (by design) changes the characteristics of knowledge and/or information by constructing a scarcity in its use, there needs to be some narrative of justification (a plausible story) to help support the legitimisation of this move. Hence, in arguments about IPRs, their recognition and their (global) governance, and in any arguments about the commodifcation of knowledge and information, these stories seldom lie far beneath the surface. Certainly these arguments can be persuasive, but equally they are no longer always accepted as self-evidently true. Rather, in the new millennium, the realm of intellectual property has become widely contested and problematic. This is not to say any of these stories is completely without merit, only that they are of less widespread applicability than hard-line supporters of the extension of the protection of IPRs may suppose or hope.

Intellectual property, global governance and computer software

Having examined the general issues that shape the realm of intellectual property, in this section I will briefly set out the wider (global) legal context that lies behind the political economy of DRM. Since 1995, IPRs have been subject to the TRIPs agreement overseen by the WTO. The agreement represents an undertaking by members of the WTO to uphold certain minimum standards of protection for IPRs and to provide legal mechanisms for their enforcement. Most importantly, the WTO's stringent dispute settlement mechanism encompasses international disputes about IPRs. Prior to 1995 there were long-standing multilateral treaties for the international recognition and protection of IPRs, overseen by the World Intellectual Property Organisation (WIPO). However, the governments of the US and various members of the EU, as well as many multinational corporations (MNCs) based in these countries, regarded these agreements as toothless in the face of 'piracy' and infringement. This prompted a number of MNCs to play a major role in the negotiations that resulted in the TRIPs agreement, drafting most of the document that became the broadly successful position advocated by the office of the US Trade Representative during the Uruguay round of multilateral trade negotiations (Sell, 2003: pp. 96–120). These companies therefore had a significant impact on the rights constituted by the TRIPs agreement.[6]

For the developed countries, TRIPs compliance has involved some legislative reorientation and occasionally new laws (or judicial reinterpretations of existing laws); for many developing countries, often with little or no tradition of IPRs, the implementation of the agreement's requirements is considerably more difficult and expensive to achieve. In recognition of these difficulties most developing country members of the WTO are currently covered by a transitional arrangement (recently extended to 2016 for pharmaceutical patents), and many have received extensive technical support (under article 67 of the agreement) to enable them to build the legal capacity to establish TRIPs compliance when they emerge from this transitional period (May, 2004). This assistance aims to reproduce global 'best practice' in the legal framework that underpins IPRs and is intended to ensure that the models of IPR-law favoured by the US and the EU are established in countries that have had different systems (or no systems) for the protection of IPRs in the past.

The TRIPs agreement builds on principles that are central to the WTO: national treatment, most-favoured nation treatment (MFN), and reciprocity. Although reciprocity does little to change the intellectual property regime (due to a long history of bilateral arrangements), the introduction of MFN (under article 4 of TRIPs) has transformed the international governance of IPRs. Most-favoured nation treatment ensures that any agreement in favour of a specific country must be extended to *all* other trading partners. Previously, under the auspices of WIPO a diverse group of conventions with different set of signatories shaped the international relations of intellectual property, alongside a complex pattern of bilateral treaties. Now, under TRIPs, and due to MFN, all undertakings apply to all members of the WTO. Furthermore, favouritism accorded domestic inventors or prospective owners of IPRs relative to non-nationals is halted; national treatment (article 3 of TRIPs) stipulates that foreign individuals and companies must be treated no worse than domestic companies. This is an important shift, as many national IPR systems had previously favoured domestic 'owners' either through legislative or procedural means.

The TRIPs agreement therefore is significant in its international extension of the rights of the owners of intellectual property. This may not immediately benefit all WTO member countries as most are net importers of IPRs, producing large flows of fees to corporations based in the US, EU and Japan. In the past, those countries that were net importers of knowledge-based products had frequently foregone protection for foreign IPRs, which allowed domestic users free access (now often called 'piracy') to these products; the US publishing industry's 'piracy' of foreign authors' works in the nineteenth century is an often-cited example. The TRIPs agreement halted this policy instrument, despite its historic success for countries ranging from Britain and the US in the nineteenth century, to the newly industrialised countries (South Korea, especially) in the second half of the twentieth century (Kumar, 2003). However, few developing country members of the WTO can withstand the political pressure deployed by the US and EU at the WTO (and bilaterally), and IPR systems across the world are converging on the TRIPs standard. While TRIPs is a complex and wide-ranging multilateral instrument, here I shall only focus on computer software as this has a direct relevance to the political economy of DRM.

Despite calls for a 'new world information and communication order' in the 1980s during the Uruguay round, the full potential of the Internet had not yet been fully appreciated. For many national negotiating teams the issue of intellectual property was seen more as an item for horse-trading and bargaining in the overall trade negotiation rather than anything that would have an immediate impact on a country's ability to access and use technologies to pursue both development and social welfare. However, since the establishment of the WTO, with TRIPs as one of the key elements of the 'single undertaking' required by all members, the control of software through IPRs has become a much more evident concern for developing countries seeking to utilise new information and communications technologies, and for those in the developed countries who reject the commodification of software (those who promote 'openness' and who play a significant role in my analysis in later chapters).

Like other elements of the TRIPs agreement, the spur towards a multilateral governance settlement for the protection of IPRs in software was initiated by US corporations. In 1980, the US Congress passed the Copyright Act that defined software programmes as literary works, and brought them under the purview of copyright. Protection was extended to operating systems including their object and source code. This entrenched a view of software as an individualised creative process (amenable to commodification), and wilfully ignored the collective processes of software development that until then had been prevalent in the industry (Halbert, 1999: pp. 52–4). The difficulty of fitting software into traditional modes of copyright subsequently suggested to some companies that patent protection might better serve their needs. Thus, in the new millennium there has been a rise in attempts to secure patents for specific software tools. However, at the time of the Uruguay round negotiations, the Japanese government managed to secure a limitation of the protection for software under TRIPs to copyright, with (software's) ideas, procedures or methods of operation and mathematical concepts excluded from the agreement (Sell, 2003: p. 114). Thus, the TRIPs agreement extended international copyright protection to cover software, as the US Congress had similarly extended the scope of US copyright fifteen years earlier.

Under article 10.1 of the TRIPs agreement, 'Computer programs, whether in source code or object code shall be protected as literary works under the Berne Convention (1971)'. The question of patents for software was left unsettled, although more recent discussions at the WIPO suggest that a future multilateral agreement extending the global protection of IPRs is likely to include patent protection for software. By protecting software under copyright, its form (as language) was given precedence over its use as tools. This allowed the longest protection period possible, and did not require registration for protection.

Conversely, the advantage of patents for software companies is that it is the function of the software that is protected, even if the actual code has been modified sufficiently to avoid copyright infringement. For the time being, however, although there may be industry pressures to recognise software patents in specific jurisdictions, and software patents *have* been established in the US, this is not currently *required* by any countries' multilateral commitments.

Therefore, in the last decade the international market for software has enjoyed the increasingly robust protection available through copyright, and as countries have become TRIPs compliant, so the ability of software companies to protect their IPRs internationally has been enhanced. This may not go as far as many would like, but nevertheless the market for software is one that is now largely patterned by IPRs. This protection has now been further enhanced by the development of technical means of protection, or DRM.

However, the legal protection of these new technologies was not firmly mandated by the TRIPs agreement, and thus in 1996 the WIPO adopted the WIPO Copyright Treaty (WCT) that, most significantly, introduced the anti-circumvention principle for DRM into the multilateral governance of IPRs. Recognising that technological fixes are seldom permanent, the WCT sought to establish a further legal layer of protection for these technologies. This legal innovation subsequently was enacted in the US Digital Millennium Copyright Act (DMCA) and the EU Copyright Directive. Both sets of legislation, among other things, made the avoidance of these technical limitations ('circumvention') illegal. Ironically, although these laws recognise that there may be a 'fair use' or 'fair dealing' argument about access to the encoded information, to gain . legal access without authorisation is rendered impossible by the complete prohibition on any modification of the technological controls with DRM programmes. This expanded legal protection underpins the effectiveness of DRM, and also serves to highlight the central problems that are the focus of the next chapter.

Notes

1. Both these latter suggestion are drawn from Scote's comments on Donna Wentworth (2005) and are suggestions for changing the discourse around this set of technologies. And while this is an interesting strategy, and one that I am in sympathy with, here I stick with DRM for clarity.
2. This section summarises various arguments drawn from May (2002: Chapters two and three) where full citations to the literature discussed can be found.
3. An extended discussion of the relevance of Marx to the discussion of the 'information age' can be found in May (2002: pp. 35–44).
4. Of less immediate relevance to the arguments about DRM, I have also argued that the claims that a shift to a new informational politics are exaggerated and the notion that the state is no longer as effective an actor in the face of the information age's technological revolution misunderstand the role of the state as the locus of regulation and the 'rule of law' that remain central to modern (globalised) capitalism (May, 2002: Chapters four and five).
5. As has been argued in Ghosh (2005), Strangelove (2005) and Weber (2004).
6. Extended discussions of the negotiations that led to TRIPs can be found in Matthews (2002: pp. 29–45) and Stewart (1993: pp. 2245–333). Space precludes a detailed treatment of TRIPs, but surveys of the agreement can be found in Matthews (2002) and May (2000). It is also worth noting that industry representatives continue to have considerable influence at the WTO, recently, for instance being part of the lobby that has been holding up Russian accession to the organisation on the basis of its weak enforcement of intellectual property rights.

2

Intellectual property and social norms

Having set out the context that broadly frames the political economy of DRM, I will now examine the relationship between the protection of IPRs and various aspects of the so-called 'new economy'. A number of problems have arisen as regards the ownership and (re)use of digital content, both in the development of new forms of electronically mediated commerce (or e-commerce) and in more long-standing sectors' use of the Internet to develop new ways of doing business. I will argue in this chapter that these problems are directly related to past (and present) social norms of consumption. Therefore, I will briefly set the question of intellectual property in its historical context, focusing on the central question of the continuing political controversies regarding the balance between private rights to reward and public goods of information dissemination and use. I will then say a little more about the manner in which intellectual property is increasingly subject to mechanisms of globalised governance, before moving to discuss the general relationship between IPRs and norms of consumption as these play out in the political economy of DRMs.

Markets, property and history

Society is not merely defined by its organisation as a capitalist society, which is to say that this is not its only characteristic, but certainly when we are thinking about market relations we cannot ignore the 'logic' of capitalism. Indeed, as I noted in Chapter one, the 'information society' and its 'new economy' remain distinctly capitalistic in organisation, whatever the claims made by some commentators. Looking back to the origins of capitalist social organisation, Karl Polanyi suggested that the idea that labour, land and money themselves might be commodities required a 'commodity fiction' to be developed during the transformation from feudalism to capitalism (Polanyi, 1944 [1957]: p. 72ff). The rendering of things not originally produced for sale as commodities required a story to be told about these resources that was not linked to their previous existence, or production, as exchangeable goods or social resources; a story needed to be told about the *normality* of organising their production and distribution through markets. In other words, things that in pre-capitalist societies had previously been socially produced and/or used, were now to be commodified; they would be sold as if their existence was based on their appearance as marketable items (as commodities), not their social utility. Land, labour and even money would no longer be the practical tools of social existence, rather they would enter (proto)capitalist markets like other commodities, and this transformation was supported through tales, or narratives, of the advantages of market relations.

This narrative of the advantages of market organisation is also central to the norms on which IPRs are founded, and continue to rely on. The narratives that were set out in Chapter one, and which underpin the justification for making knowledge and information into property, are centred upon the argument that societies need markets if they are to reward, protect and use efficiently the knowledge and information that individuals may develop. While in other cases markets pre-existed capitalism, for the proto-capitalist organisation of markets in knowledge and/or information, (legitimated) commodification was required because otherwise the markets themselves could not be established (May, 2007). Thus, as soon as early proto-capitalists sought to arrange opportunities for the accumulation of surpluses through the production of goods encompassing knowledge and/or information for sale, then they required the legal structures of (early) intellectual property if the knowledge/informational element was to contribute significantly to the price obtained. In other words, where profit (and hence accumulation) was dependent to a greater extent on the informational content of the product, IPRs were required (to a greater extent) to halt unauthorised duplication. Once a technique, technology, or a form of content, has been exchanged, without some enforced legal scarcity, competing providers or manufacturers could utilise the knowledge element of the commodity but under-cut the original supplier, reducing their profits (and hence their rate of capital accumulation), as these competitors did not need to recover the initial costs of developing the idea/technique.

Markets can exist for tangible/material goods that appear similar to their later capitalist counterparts (although of course the social relations they encompass are very different), and indeed many goods were extensively traded through pre-capitalist markets. However, for a market to exist in 'intellectual products' new rights of ownership needed to be imposed, as they had not been established alongside previous mechanisms for dealing with the distribution and transfer of scarce (material) goods. Certainly, intellectual elements had been incorporated into pre-capitalist market exchanged goods, but no legal rights were accorded this element over and above the early ownership rights that allowed some form of market exchange. Thus, while in other areas of nascent capitalist economic relations, pre-capitalist and capitalist-produced goods could be traded in the same market without an obvious distinction being drawn (and thus capitalist developments were more gradual), for 'intellectual products' (proto)capitalists themselves *constructed* a new market.

The mercantilist policy of knowledge and technology capture, typified by the Renaissance use of national (or territorially limited) patent systems to encourage the importation of valuable technologies and techniques explicitly for the purposes of strategic economic development, underpinned proto-capitalist accumulation strategies (May and Sell, 2005: Chapter three). Later campaigns by groups such as the Stationers and various inventors' groups for their property to be recognised in new technologies or texts consolidated this move to early capitalism. This was a particularly European process, and as such it is of little surprise to see the states that have been identified as those that carried the establishment of capitalist social relations forward, namely Venice, then Britain, are those where intellectual property was most swiftly developed.

The 'knowledge commons', from which intellectual property has temporarily rendered certain 'items' as scarce property, were implicitly recognised as soon as early forms of intellectual property were codified in the Renaissance. Limits on the period of protection (making IPRs temporary) were used to put socially useful knowledge back into these commons. This recognised that many aspects of 'new' knowledge were actually drawn from the existing pool of information and knowledge represented by the commons, and thus the continued vitality of the commons was also crucial for continuing innovation and creativity. Extraction from these commons was originally (in the sixteenth to eighteenth centuries) regarded as a privilege accorded only in certain circumstances; duties such as training in the practices covered, or the use of the technologies towards specific ends, were part of the grant of temporary monopoly. Thus, in Venice the monopoly on the supply of reading glasses included the requirement that the monopoly holder train apprentices in their production (and therefore allowed for the expansion of supply once the monopoly had expired).

However, the subsequent history of intellectual property has seen these monopoly grants gain the status of rights with few, if any, responsibilities attached (May and Sell, 2005). As the centuries passed, so the idea of making property from knowledge and information became more normal and accepted. With this acceptance came the gradual, and in the twentieth century, accelerated, widening of the scope of that which might be included in the regime of ownership and protection that has become known as intellectual property (itself a term that has only entered common usage in the last 100 years). These rights construct a scarcity of legitimate use which is far from natural, and indeed by limiting the use of such properties on the basis of wealth (by extracting a price for use) can hardly be said to be self-evidently to the benefit of all members of society. Therefore, significant time and effort is spent telling stories about intellectual property that are meant to justify its existence as a set of legal rights.

Scarcity, withholding and the global 'problem' of intellectual property

The construction of scarcity (of use) through the commodification of knowledge plays a vital role in the operation of contemporary global capitalism, but considerable effort is required to support the argument that such scarcity is socially beneficial. The problem is that when the recognition of property rights is co-existent with scarce resources, then, as John Commons noted eighty years ago, 'the mere holding of property becomes a power to withhold, far beyond that which either the labourer has over his labour or the investor has over his savings, and beyond anything known when this power was being perfected by the early common law or early business law' (Commons, 1924 [1959]: p. 53). This is because the use of property (in its various forms – from land to machines) allows us to generate the wealth/income that underpins our own wellbeing; our ability to labour is useless, if we lack the property to apply our efforts to. This is even more pronounced when the scarcity itself is legally constituted through the imposition of intellectual property rights to restrain use which naturally is not so constrained. It is this move from holding to *withholding*, the ability to restrict use, which is of crucial importance in the political economy of IPRs, and which has been the most important political (and practical) issue raised by DRM technologies or tools. When resources are potentially freely available and inexhaustible (as is knowledge) then the imposition of property rights, and the mechanical denial of access, introduces this scarcity and establishes significant social and political power as regards the benefits from use.

Conventionally when intellectual property is eulogised, it is on the basis of the protection of the creator, the owner of such knowledge which is made property. Their rights are protected so as to act as a general spur to innovation and socially useful activity. Arguments about just desserts and selfhood are allied to the need for social efficiency in the allocation of resources. However, Jeremy Waldron argues all this talk of property 'sounds a lot less pleasant if... we turn the matter around and say we are imposing *duties*, restricting *freedom* and inflicting *burdens* on certain individuals for the sake of the greater social good' (Waldron, 1993: 862). At least part of the problem may be the over-emphasis of the second term at the expense of the first when discussing 'intellectual property'; while the latter stresses legitimate control through widely respected ideas of 'ownership', the former encompasses notions of access to knowledge (Patterson, 2001: 707). This is to say that IPRs limit the actions of others regarding knowledge vis-à-vis the owners of intellectual property, and as such non-owners are being forced to sacrifice their particular wants or needs for a potentially inexhaustible resource on the alter of social necessity.

Non-owners' 'rights' are constrained because these rights are regarded as less important in law than the support of the social good of innovation by IPRs, or perhaps more accurately the *property* rights of owners are being privileged over the *political* rights of users. However, in the legal realm in which DRMs are most often deployed, current copyright legislation across the world, and the history of such legislation, has not usually privileged the creators' rights (whatever the rhetoric) but rather has been concerned to secure the rights of the agents (companies) responsible for commodification (Macmillan, 2002). Thus, the rhetoric of individual rights is mobilised on behalf of corporate entities, who receive protections legitimated not on the basis of their own (commercial) character, but derived from a narrative of individual human endeavour. Just to be clear that it is the commercial issue that is the key issue: when tribal groups and indigenous populations (as collectives) have tried to claim intellectual property rights (in traditional knowledge, for example), the legal regime of IPRs has not merely had great difficulty in recognising these claims, but until recently many such claims were actually forthrightly and successfully resisted by lawyers and companies who had benefited from the non-recognition of such property (especially in the realm of bio-resources).[1]

For those suffering the social costs of the withholding of information or knowledge, political action in the past has often (at least partially) succeeded in (re)balancing private rights and public benefits to produce new settlements as regards IPRs in national jurisdictions. Therefore, when the justifications mobilised to underpin the protection of IPRs were based on a cosmopolitan entity (a relatively coherent society) delimited by national jurisdiction, the inherent problems with commodifying knowledge could be (at least partly) relieved through legal amendment (or social values promoted through the use of judicial precedent) in response to national political pressure and representations. However under the TRIPs agreement, and other post-TRIPs treaties that increasingly shape domestic legislation across the world, while these cosmopolitan narratives have been used to produce a global legal settlement for IPRs the political mechanisms which can address the social effects on user communities remain relatively under-developed. The implicit cosmopolitanism of the narratives of justification that are suffused throughout the TRIPs agreement, and the latter WIPO Copyright Treaty, are not matched by a similarly scaled (global) polity; although IPR-laws assume a society which can seek to balance private rights and public benefits, the political method for articulating such a public interest is almost entirely absent at the global level.

Despite this relatively under-developed (global) polity, these multilateral agreements are far from uncontested, with significant political mobilisation in the last decade focusing on the difficulties and inequalities that are fostered by the emergence of a global regulatory regime for IPRs. This has centred on the position that the current (TRIPs engendered) globalised social bargain between private rewards and public benefits is not universally appropriate, although it continues to inform post-TRIPs multilateral governance of intellectual property. In its contemporary globalised form, this bargain privileges the rights of owners (predominantly domiciled in rich, developed countries) and downplays or marginalises the social costs (and curtailed public benefits) widely experienced in developing countries. However, even in the developed countries themselves, there is a clear division between the privileged interests of the IPR-controlling companies in any specific sector and those who seek to access or use these products or services.

While not entirely absent from the rhetoric around IPRs, the public interest is only recognised in this governance regime as a *residual* after *all* other possible rights have been exercised. Any public regarding aspect of IPRs is subsumed beneath the normative narratives of individual rights that are central to this regime of intellectual property. However, the notion that what we might term 'access rights' are merely exceptions (and thus can increasingly be regarded as a residual when all private rights have been exercised) misunderstands the historical construction of copyright (Hoeren, 2003; May and Sell, 2005). Rather, copyright should be understood as being embedded in a complex relationship with other (public regarding) rights, such as freedom of expression, freedom of information, and the right to the availability of socially useful and important knowledge to those who could benefit from it.

This has led to the argument that there is a real need to (again) recognise the political character of the balance between private rewards and public benefits that has been central to the legal history of IPRs in national legislation.

Without a well-developed global society able to mediate between private rewards and social goods/public benefits, the notion of a global regime for IPRs is currently difficult (if not impossible) to justify. Within the developed countries, and between them and the lesser developed regions of the global system, significant tensions have therefore arisen between 'owners' and 'users' over the morality of the recognition of property rights in knowledge and information.

To sum up, we might say that the global governance of IPRs reflects the depiction of the contemporary (global) polity suggested by Richard Higgott and Morten Ougaard. While there is a 'thick interconnectedness' between 'political structures, agents and process, with transnational properties', these are as yet only linked by a 'thin community that transcends the territorial state' (Higgott and Ougaard, 2002: p. 12). The current global governance of intellectual property (encompassing the TRIPs agreement, the WCT and other post-TRIPs mechanisms), alongside the international (industry-based) lobbying groups involved in establishing and expanding the (specific) agenda of IPR-governance, all fit with the notion of 'thick interconnectedness'. Not only via the Internet (which itself is very unevenly globalised) but also through the use of new (patented) technologies, the increasingly globalised reach of brands and the increasingly global consumption of copyrighted products, the *globalised* interconnectivity of the political economy of knowledge commodification becomes more pronounced by the day. However, there remains only a 'thin community' as regards the socio-political justification of IPRs on which the governance regime is founded, and no real mechanisms (previously encoded in domestic law) to recognise the social values (and social costs) of this (putative, global) community.

We should recall that before the end of the nineteenth century (and for many countries, into the twentieth), non-national intellectual property was seldom recognised at all. Famously, the US book trade thrived in the nineteenth century publishing 'unauthorised' works of European authors, only recognising the rights of non-US authors in 1891. But perhaps less often noted, US industrialisation proceeded apace with technologies that were patented abroad, but freely available (through 'piracy') to entrepreneurs in America, especially in the petrochemical sector (a model followed by both India and China, for instance). As Peter Gakunu noted before TRIPs had even been finally negotiated, in the past:

> ... perhaps the developmental aspects of intellectual property were more interesting to the United States than the trade aspects are at the present time. Now that the United States is at its present level of technological development, the trade aspects of intellectual property become more important for it than the development aspects. (Gakunu, 1989: 364)

Certainly, the discourse privileging trade interests in IPR-protection has almost completely drowned out development and/or public good-related interests and concerns at both the international and national levels. For many developing countries, trade issues are secondary to the more pressing need to access information and knowledge that will support their further economic development.

The world is not sufficiently *evenly* globalised (whatever commentators celebrating the 'borderless world' claim) for any political and legal settlement to closely follow previous national political bargains, because the array of social interests at the global level is significantly different to those in those countries where IPR-related legislation was originally developed. The justifications that have previously been used to underpin IPRs do not have sufficient purchase on the current global situation without a mechanism for recognising the social costs or down-side of any 'bargain' which promotes private rewards. As Graeme Dinwoodie stresses:

> ... the incorporation of intellectual property agreements within trade mechanisms might (if trade concerns become paramount) deprive intellectual property policymaking of the rich palette of *human values* that historically has influenced its formulation. Considering only the ability to exploit comparative advantage in the ownership of intellectual property rights would appear to make international intellectual property policy less multi-dimensional. (Dinwoodie, 2002: 1004; emphasis added)

It is this lack of multidimensionality, indeed the frequent absence of consideration of non-commercial *human* values, that is the key problem. The vast inequalities evident in the world are not recognised when the social costs that are required for the continued support of private rewards remain largely hidden in multilateral policy discussions. Into this realm of contested norms and disputes over the scope of IPRs, DRM attempts to establish certainty of control for owners through technological rather than through (exclusively) legal means.

Digital rights management, the norms of copyright, and the commons

Although information and knowledge could always be controlled by keeping it secret, and theft could be punished under common law by virtue of the recognition of the 'ownership' of trade secrets, most often to make a profit from knowledge it has had to be shared or used in some way. This was no less the case in the emergent realm of computerisation in the 1970s: in the same way that keeping the contents of a book secret would not enable it to be reproduced and sold to large numbers of willing customers, marketing software to consumers outside the originating organisation meant that access to the workings, or content, of the software became possible (if not necessary – less technologically-adept users could just use the software with little idea about its inner workings). Thus, while large-scale mainframe computing had involved bespoke, single-purchaser software, which could then be protected as a trade secret by its owner, once software started to become a more commodity-like product the characteristics of its ownership and sale shifted significantly.

Most of these large-scale computers included file permission/access control systems that allowed different levels of access to differently identified individual users in a multi-user system; nominated users could copy, while others could not. Once software started to be distributed on floppy discs to early users of personal computers (PCs), the problem of unauthorised copies of software being produced by others than the original vendors was quickly recognised. This initially prompted the use of scare-tactics threatening legal action against infringers (usually stickers on the software packaging), and then a move to encrypted files (Rosenblatt, Trippe and Mooney, 2002: p. xi). Thus, expensive but easily copied software (most obviously type fonts) swiftly started to be distributed using encrypted systems, which, while not unbreakable, certainly deterred casual and 'accidental' infringement. However, these systems were not popular – not least among institutional customers who needed to make copies for back-up should systems fail, and to distribute software within the organisation as required, but also among independent users for similar reasons. Indeed, when Borland International offered a copy-protected version of its Sidekick software for a 30.00 USD discount on the price of the unlimited use version, the more expensive version without copy-protection outsold the cheaper version by a margin of five to one (Rothchild, 2005: 547). Thus, the attempts to produce an early form of DRM did not fare well; after a quite extensive initial roll-out of copy-protected software, and a large number of user complaints regarding its inconvenience, the practice was largely halted and software went back to being distributed on floppy discs with little or no copy-protection.

However, once the Internet started to spread out beyond its initial academic set of users in the early 1990s, a number of vendors again started to become (perhaps understandably) worried that once one unauthorised copy had been produced it could spread across the Internet, severely undermining their ability to sell 'original' copies of software (or content). These worries prompted IBM to produce a protection package called *infoMarket*, which combined a cryptographic programme (Cryptolope) that governed access to software products and a linked system that facilitated the establishment of an Internet-mediated market in these products. Taking a different approach, around the same time Electronic Publishing Resources developed a system (often referred to as 'dongles') that combined software distribution with dedicated hardware that allowed use to be controlled (Rosenblatt, Trippe and Mooney, 2002: p. xii). However, an 'arms race' promptly emerged between those seeking to protect their property and those seeking to access or use digital products/tools without authorisation from the owner (Stefik, 1999: p. 57ff). The result was that, quite quickly, it became clear that for these systems to work not only did they have to be extensively deployed, but that the possible circumvention of the system itself needed to be made illegal.

Thus, at the prompting of the content and software industries (that had already been successful in pushing through the TRIPs agreement), a number of national delegations at the World Intellectual Property Organisation managed to include the issue of circumvention in the negotiations over the WIPO's so-called 'Internet treaties'. When in 1996 the WIPO adopted the WIPO Copyright Treaty (WCT), significantly, the anti-circumvention principle was recognised in the multilateral governance of IPRs for the first time (Drahos and Braithwaite, 2002: p. 184). Legal measures to 'protect' digital rights management software from unauthorised technical interventions have subsequently been included in regional (EU) and national (US; UK) legislation,[2] while many developing countries are also under pressure to adopt similar legislation.

The WCT includes under articles 11 and 12 significant measures as regards the introduction of DRM technologies and their enforcement as IPR-related technological solutions to 'piracy', although the form of implementation of such requirements itself remains a national issue. This brings us to the specific problem that is at the centre of the analysis set out in this book; the impact on the political economy of knowledge and information of the deployment of DRM technologies. Although the introduction of legal protection for DRM is intended to (further) protect the rights of intellectual property owners, recognising that technological fixes are seldom permanent, the WCT also sought to establish a further legal layer of protection for these technologies by making circumvention of technical anti-copying measures illegal. It is this combination of technological measures with a legal prohibition on their circumvention that has proved so contentious, as we will see.

The United States Congress passed the Digital Millennium Copyright Act (DMCA) in 1998, as enabling legislation for the WIPO copyright treaty. The software and entertainment industry, music and film associations, lobbied very hard for protection of works disseminated on the Internet (and via other digital carriers, such as CDs), prevailing over the vociferous opposition of public interest advocates such as librarians, law professors, and electronic civil liberties activists (Vaidhyanathan, 2001: p. 175; Yu, 2004: 910). As with the negotiation of the TRIPs agreement during the Uruguay round of multilateral trade talks, the content industries managed to shape legislation to broadly reflect their interests. However, the protections enshrined in US legalisation go beyond even those measures actually required by their multilateral treaty commitments (Rice, 2002: 121; Jeanneret, 2002: 164). To some extent this explains why the issue has been more widely debated in the US than elsewhere.

The debates around the DMCA in the US have already demonstrated that the use of DRM technology, and its legal protection, may represent a more generalised and major challenge for 'fair use' across the world as it becomes more widely deployed. Although the UK Copyright Designs and Patents act of 1988, for instance, would seem to offer similar protection to DRM technologies, this has been subject to considerably less comment, which may tell us something about the dominance of US-related issues on the Internet, as well as the more litigious character of US business (which has made the issue more obvious to the consuming public).

The DMCA itself offers broad protection for digital works. It prohibits circumvention of any technological protection against copying and prevents the production of any device or provision of any service designed to defeat protection mechanisms. As Robert Merges has pointed out, by directly prohibiting the use of specific technologies, 'the protection of expression' is now 'achieved through the regulation of devices' (Merges, 2000: 2202); protection of rights has been rendered as technical rather than legal, and therefore, for the first time in the US as Siva Vaidyanathan argues, the law 'puts the power to regulate copying in the hands of engineers and the companies that employ them. It takes the decision-making power away from Congress, courts, librarians, writers, artists, and researchers' (Vaidhyanathan, 2001: p. 174). Critics have charged that these provisions go too far, reflect too little knowledge of the complex history of copyright provisions, and constrict activities that were once considered to be fair use.[3]

For example, even though teachers can use copyrighted material for educational purposes under the doctrine of fair use, since the enactment of the DMCA this has often become technically impossible in the US. Teachers are unable to incorporate copyrighted material into a PowerPoint presentation for students, as the copy protection measures the content industries have made legally insurmountable ensure any such inclusion is technically very difficult. Furthermore, the DMCA makes any attempt to circumvent this copy protection a criminal offence, even when the intended use is considered 'fair use' under historical definitions (Marlin-Bennett, 2004: p. 86). The content industries also have used the DMCA to prevent the dissemination of information about circumventing encryption technologies, as publicising methods of circumventing DRM software can itself be illegal even where this is discussed in a scholarly forum (Yu, 2004: 911–12). Content providers praise this expanded protection, although they complain that it is difficult to enforce (Marlin-Bennett, 2004: p. 85), while for users a set of rights to 'fair use' that had been developed and consolidated over time have been withdrawn with little or any political recourse or meaningful discussion.

The use of DRM, and its legal enforcement, can therefore represent a major challenge for previous practices (and precedents) regarding 'fair use' or in European terms 'fair-dealing'. However, while the debates have been wide-ranging and very public in the US, in Europe the enaction of the European Copyright Directive (EUCD) seems to have prompted much less public outcry.[4] However, in line with the DMCA, the EUCD prohibits the circumvention of technological measures of protection that are instigated by copyright holders ('owners'), irrespective of the reasons for such circumvention (i.e. even if it to establish uses that are legal; article 6). However, under article 6.4, a wide-ranging list of exceptions from these limitations are carried forward as regards various public-regarding uses and certain public institutions. While these exceptions are not mandatory and may be in tension with the absolute prohibition on circumvention, considerable potential for litigation and dispute is introduced by this attempt to continue the variable 'fair dealing'/'fair use' doctrines of previous copyright legislation. While there has been much less political debate and criticism levelled at the EUCD, equally it has not been widely adopted across Europe, even though the intent was that it would be fully implemented by the end of 2002.

Norms vs. technology

It seems likely that the deployment of DRM technologies will consolidate (or even worsen) the uneven distribution of information and knowledge across the so-called 'digital divide'. This is most obvious in the collapse of the generally-accepted social norms of content usage. On one side, content users have utilised technology that they have purchased legally to 'infringe' the rights of content owners (of which the use of MP3 files, and their Internet mediated 'sharing' through various peer-to-peer technologies, is only the most obvious example); on the other, content 'owners' have actually expanded the potential scope of their rights (relative to previous settlements), most clearly by halting certain collective practices (copying and thereby sharing) that previously existed as (tacit) rights for consumers to use goods as they saw fit, provided this was not for commercial gain. Utilising click-through terms and conditions on websites offering legal digital material, as Jerome Reichman and Paul Uhlir point out: 'users must accede to non-negotiable electronic contracts, which impose the copyright owner's terms and conditions without regard to the traditional defences and statutory immunities of copyright law' (Reichman and Uhlir, 2003: 378). Therefore, one of the key elements of the 'problem' of DRM technologies is the solidification of aspects of copyright law that have hitherto been indeterminate at the margins, with areas of legal greyness amenable to politics and diplomacy circumscribed or removed.

This is to say that previously, the assertion of ownership (and thereby control over use) had been managed through the effective incompleteness of such claims, and the recognition of certain 'fair use' of rights-bearing works. In the past, and for most of the twentieth century, there was a grey area rather than a sharp division between owners' rights and theft; there was a realm of tacit acceptance of formally illegal activity. This area at the edge of the realm of IPRs' coverage, which was largely unenforced as regards owners' 'rights', still lay within the realm of formally-established legal protection owners might expect if they pushed their rights to the legal limit. However, for most industries a tacit acceptance of 'piracy' or 'leakage', while this was of relatively minor extent, meant that such limits to protection were seldom claimed.

For example, in the last quarter of the twentieth century, despite claims that 'home taping is killing music', the music industry accepted home compilations and a gift economy of private cassette tapes as beyond the realm of their ability to control. This acceptance was a reflection of the clearly degenerative copying technologies then available to home consumers. Similarly, for book publishers, photocopying may certainly have eaten into some sales but photocopying whole books, while sometimes undertaken, was at such an expense of time and money (copying was hardly a cheap option) that little real effort was expended tracking down individual 'pirates' (copy-shops on university campuses were another matter, and have been vigorously prosecuted for mass production of photocopied editions of expensive texts). In both cases, the serial copying of 'pirated' copies led to such quality shortcomings that the central reproduction technology retained its advantages. However, digitisation has changed this state of affairs.

Digitisation has removed the quality/copy trade-off by allowing multigenerational copies to be, for all intents and purposes, exact copies of the original digital artefact, and thus the monopoly on high quality reproduction has been removed from authorised distribution channels. A 'frictionless environment' for content, where successive copies do not degrade (Scott, 2001) immediately raises the potential threat that once a digital good is distributed, unauthorised copies can compete throughout its market for consumer use. And whereas in the past the users of copied goods would receive an inferior product, and thus the price discrimination between authorised and unauthorised copies was clearly reflected in the quality of product, digital copies have removed this distinction. In a very real sense there was a social norm that linked high quality reproduction to legal consumption, and the acceptance of low levels of reproduction with illegal copies, and clearly maintained the advantages of legal consumption.

The speed of technological advancement in the realm of digital copying 'forced' the content industries to respond (Kim, 2003: 97), but this also meant that the previously legitimated political processes for (re)balancing private and public rights/benefits were left behind in the scramble for protection. This rush for protection also reflected the perceived challenge that these new technologies presented for existing business models in the content industries. Indeed, the clear possibility of removing the inter-mediation between producers and audience that digital distribution promised, challenged the very role that the content industries have built their profits upon (Lucchi, 2005: 1117–8). Thus, it should be no surprise that the content industries were at the forefront of the establishment of DRM software, and were voracious in their desire to see it legally protected from circumvention.

However, and very importantly, as Jessica Litman has argued, copyright laws 'never gave copyright owners rights as expansive as those they have recently argued were their due' during debates around the 'copyright problem' on-line (Litman, 2001: p. 114). This is to say that copyright holders have never been granted the almost complete control over use that now seems to be claimed; in the past, once sold the use of the copyrighted item and its subsequent re-use were not subject to any real control. Indeed, as Lydia Pallas Loren notes:

> The law has never granted copyright owners an absolute monopoly. Instead, the laws strike a balance between granting a certain level of protection and

> guaranteeing a certain level of access and use. The unregulated implementation of technological protection measures enables content providers to obtain protections the law does not afford. Technological protection systems can and should be employed by copyright owners to capture rights permitted by copyright law. The law, however, needs to guard against the use of technological protection systems to capture rights not permitted by copyright law. (Loren, 2002: 143)

The move to enact measures like the DMCA has not reflected the balance of interests that copyright laws slowly established over a long political history, but does reflect the dynamic of this history (claims for rights contesting with claims for access). This is another attempt, facilitated by technological advances, to expand the rights of one specific interest, the owners, with little regard for the diminution of the other interests accorded weight by copyright in the past: the public or social good of access.

The report by the Commission on IPRs (commissioned by the British Department for International Development) concluded that for developing countries, 'where Internet connectivity is limited and subscriptions to on-line resources unaffordable, [DRM technologies] may exclude access to these materials altogether and impose a heavy burden that will delay the participation of those countries in the global knowledge-based society' (CIPR, 2002: p. 106).[5] The extra controls that subscription on-line services and copy-protected products allow content owners dissipate the hard-won compromises for users which have been encapsulated by previous understandings of 'fair use' or 'fair dealing', and while the Internet may be increasing the potential access to global knowledge and information resources,

DRM undermines and compromises such possibilities in many areas of commercial information dissemination.

Lawrence Lessig has argued that DRM and other linked control technologies may also allow powerful industries to 'leverage' their control of 'real' markets into a control of 'virtual' markets on the Internet (Lessig, 2001: p. 200, and passim). This is not to say Lessig is necessarily arguing against copyright or other forms of IPRs, rather he is concerned about the likely re-orientation of IPRs' balance between private rights and public goods. As he notes, recently IPR regimes have expanded beyond their initial justification (as encapsulated in law) to produce market constraints beyond the immediate realm of intellectual property, but such restrictions 'are artificial ... they simply benefit one person at the expense of another ... [But] if they limit the range of creativity by virtue of the system of control they erect, why do we have them?' (Lessig, 2001: p. 217).[6] Indeed, this normative problem reveals that the questions around DRM technologies are not questions of technical efficacy and cost, but rather the problem of mediating clashing interests in a relatively new technological realm.

Therefore, at least as regards the manner in which fair-use is understood, the key difference concerns the way that any rights of unencumbered public access are conceived. On the one hand, for supporters of DRM, most obviously in the content industries (music and text) and those who wish to see the control of intellectual property consolidated, doctrines of fair use were never more than a tacit recognition that rights to halt or control copying and use were unenforceable at the margins. Now, DRM software allows owners finally to properly control and shape usage in their own interests as they have always been promised by the law. On the other hand, those who support public access rights (such as the UK National Consumer Council or the Electronic Frontier

Foundation) see the issue of fair use as directly linked to copyright's public purpose, and as having its roots with the recognition that any intellectual property rights carve rights out of a potential public realm of knowledge. Here, fair use is not merely a tacit recognition of regulatory (or market) failure, but rather a positive right of access that needs to be protected and articulated through the law.

The legitimisation of IPRs, as laid out in the extensively-used narratives of justification I mentioned at the beginning of this book, assumes that property rights in knowledge serve a set of social goods. Chief among these is that social advance is served by the innovation and creation that copyright (as well as patents and other forms of IPRs) supports. While these justifications stress private rights, they have also always implied a 'knowledge commons' that is enlarged by the temporary enclosure of knowledge to encourage further intellectual activity. The control of content that DRM allows produces two clear problems in the enforcement of IPRs. Firstly, the breakdown of the mediated settlement over IPRs seems to be prompting a form of 'blowback', already evident in the music industry. The desire of 'owners' to enact monopoly controls has led content users to become more cynical about *perceived* profiteering, and hence the rhetoric of responsible consumption (allied to the narratives of private rewards) has started to crumble.

Secondly, a disjuncture has opened up between the society in which rights are protected and the society in which users' costs are evident. In many national jurisdictions there remains a chance that public and/or political opinion can be mobilised either to restrain the actual enforcement of rights and their scope, or to (re)establish 'fair-use' through legal means as a recognition of the continued needs of the public realm. Furthermore, in national jurisdictions the bargain between private rights and public access has an easily discernible pay-off: the society involved reaps the benefits of innovation and creativity. In the global realm, however, given the extremes of economic inequality, alongside necessarily diffused user communities, the rewards flow to a relatively closed group while the social advantages of advances may be limited by the constrictions put on use of content goods. These problems represent a breakdown in the social, or normative, bargain that has previously underpinned the recognition, use, and acceptance of IPRs.

Where poor groups are excluded from use to important intellectual resources (for example, those carried in medical databases), access to ascertain any fair-use demands may not be possible (i.e. they may not be able to discover what specific content-goods might serve their needs without first paying for them). This has led Ruth Okediji (2000) to argue that although there are some aspects of 'fair-use' that can still be discovered within TRIPs, such provisions are fragmented and unsatisfactory. She argues that an 'international fair-use doctrine' is required that would better reflect the explicit objective of article 7 of TRIPs, expressing the agreement's support for national legislation that balances rights *and* obligations. The case of DRM technology (and its legal support through the WCT) demonstrates the power of technological innovations to disrupt the legal settlements around IPRs, and certainly as with other past innovations in content distribution from print to video recording, there is likely to be a period where the previous balance between private rights and public benefits (or social use) remains disrupted before political process produces, through a series of explicit and implicit negotiations, a newly legitimated balance. However, in the post-TRIPs world the political process and deliberation (at the WTO or elsewhere) may be seriously truncated due to the wholesale shift in the balance of rights and obligations, and the tension between global regulation and national political deliberative processes.

Surrendering to digital rights management?

One of the key drivers to deploy DRM is the removal of the area of greyness which had allowed some flexibility in the public/private balance for IPRs; DRM technologies were intended to shore up private rights and finally make them reflect the rights that, it was claimed, had been encoded for years in IPR laws. These legal rights, that had been difficult to enforce at the margins, would now be encoded in technologies that made infringement very difficult. Moreover, protection would be less reliant on unevenly recognised social norms of content use, such as those underpinned by the narratives of justification for IPR protection; even those who *did* believe the stories that are told to justify IPRs would have their behaviour constrained. However, at the same time the deployment of DRM has also made the private inroads into the public realm much more obvious by removing the mediated area older technologies had left as a 'buffer-zone' or grey area between contending interests over knowledge and information usage.

In addition, the use of DRM reverses the burden of proof. Selena Kim sums up the issue well:

> In the analogue world, people go ahead and use the work if they believe themselves entitled to do so. It is only if users are sued for infringement that they invoke the relevant copyright exception as defence. In a digital world encapsulated by access control and with embedded copy control, a potential user of a work may have to ask for permission twice: once to access a work, and again to

copy an excerpt. The exception to copyright is not being put forward as a defence; it is put forward to show entitlement to use the work. (Kim, 2003: 112)

There are two problems immediately apparent: the first political, the second technical. Firstly, the assumption is that private rights are privileged and thus public access is in the gift of the owner, which represents a significant denial of the role of the public domain; secondly, by making such requests explicit and user driven, owners may be swamped by requests (producing delays that will negatively impact on the utility gained by use), while users may be dissuaded at the margins from using certain informational resources due to the process of requesting permissions. Generally, then, there may be a 'chilling' effect on the use of copyrighted materials.

Siva Vaidhyanathan, discussing the DMCA, but with wider relevance, suggests that this reorientation of the legal institution of IPRs represents 'four surrenders':

1. The surrender of balance to control ... content providers can set the terms for access to and use of a work. There is no balance if the copyright owner has all the power;

2. The surrender of public interest to private interest. The rhetoric of 'intellectual property' in the 1990s was punctuated by appeals to prevent theft and efforts to extend markets. There was little public discussion about copyright as a public good that can encourage a rich public sphere and diverse democratic culture;

3. The surrender of republican [sic] deliberation within the nation-state to unelected multilateral non-governmental bodies ...;

4. The surrender of culture to technology ...
[previously] copyright was a public bargain
between producers and users. It was democratically
negotiated, judicially mediated and often messy
and imperfect. Now the very presence of even
faulty technology trumps any public interest in
fair use and open access. (Vaidhyanathan, 2001:
pp. 159–60)

These 'four surrenders' have removed the grey area that
allowed the contradictions between the fully expressed
'needs' of rights holders and public (or social) users to remain
unformalised, leaving a seemingly unresolvable conflict as a
major problem within intellectual property politics.

The privileging of owners' interests has a long history in
the wider realm of intellectual property, but for the first time
owners have been able to secure their rights not merely via
legal limits on use (which have always been incompletely
enforced), but through the limitation of the actual
possibilities of technologies. Whereas in the past, limitations
were in line with the possible uses of technological
deployment, the instigation of DRM has involved limiting
the already existing technological capacity for distribution.
This has been linked to the reorientation of the knowledge
commons, or public domain, to be only that which remains
once all private rights have been exercised; it has gone from
a positive good in its own right, to merely a residual
repository. Thus, although much information is available
freely on the Internet, much of this is only available because
potential owners have *decided* not to exercise their rights
through technical limitations on access; material is available
through goodwill, and could be as easily withdrawn at any
time, rather that available as a right beyond personal or
corporate whim. While Vaidhyanathan is right that there is

a shift in political deliberation (towards relatively unaccountable international/multilateral governance mechanisms), the more important shift is the attempt to render politics null and void through the imposition of technology.

The central role of IPRs is to construct a scarcity as regards use where none necessarily exists in the realm of information and knowledge. Fair use (like term limits under patent law) has historically recognised that sometimes this is bought at too great a social cost and thus limits the monopoly rights enjoyed by the 'owner' by allowing some non-remunerated 'fair use'. Or as Glynn Lunney sums it up:

> Once we acknowledge the public good character of copyrighted works, then, from an economic perspective, fair use must necessarily balance, on one hand, the potential public benefit of additional or better works from prohibiting the use at issue, and on the other, the potential public benefit from the use itself. In applying this balance ... we should consider directly what the public has to gain and what it has to lose for the use at issue given today's technology and associated market structures. Under this balancing approach, a use should be found unfair and hence infringing only where the copyright owner has proven by the preponderance of the evidence that society has more to gain than it has to lose by prohibiting the use at issue. (Lunney, 2002: 1030)

While this might involve some arguments about the burden of proof and how such claims could be established, it also allows for a consideration of whether potential damages and future possible losses might be discounted and actual current usage benefits privileged. This balancing may have been pursued in the past (although even then this is probably exaggerating the public benefits captured by fair use as regards previous content distribution technologies), but digital rights management will have (and is already having) the effect of shifting this posited private/public bargain firmly in the direction of greater protection of 'owners' rights, with a considerable diminution of social rights of public access, and an effective denial of any process of re-balancing.

Notes

1. This is largely the result of corporations' success in achieving recognition for themselves as individuals under law (able to benefit from rights accorded to 'natural persons'), see the discussion of the history of this development in company law in May (2006b).
2. A comprehensive guide to the legislative changes made by the EU, Australia, Japan and the US in response to the WIPO treaty can be found in Kim (2003), which, however, rather optimistically concludes: 'Hopefully, in the future, with decreased transaction costs and an efficient way to deal with access to works, there will be fewer problems [regarding 'fair use' access to DRM protected files]' (Kim, 2003: 119). I am not so sure.
3. For the long history of copyright see May and Sell (2005), and for a recent brief discussion of these issues see Chang (2005: 241–6).
4. Although organisations from the National Consumer Council to Free Culture UK have been raising these issues in various forums, most of the press and media coverage of this issue in the UK takes the industry view as normal and the criticisms (in most cases) as merely interesting 'balance'.
5. See also Electronic Frontier Foundation (2006b).
6. In March 2006, Lessig welcomed 'Sun's efforts to rally the community around the development of open source, royalty

free DRM standards that support "fair-use" and that don't block the development of Creative Commons ideals' (see *http://biz.yahoo.com/prnews/060321/sftu071.html?.v=46*). While it remains to be seen what the standards developed look like, it could as easily be the case that this would ensure the expansion of DRM-related restrictions bringing about exactly the sort of over-arching environment of control that Lessig fears.

3

Digital rights management: two trajectories

In the first two chapters I have discussed the question of digital rights management (DRM) technologies in rather general terms, and briefly related it to some contemporary questions raised by the protection of intellectual property. In this chapter I examine in more detail the two main types of DRM that have been developed, which I have termed 'hard' DRM and 'soft' DRM. These are ideal types at opposite ends of a continuum between which most actual forms of DRMs lie, and as such are not intended as descriptions of actual DRM tools, but rather as devices to establish the range of issues that will be explored in the rest of the book. Below, I set out each form's ideal typical character and method of rights' protection, along with some illustrations. I also examine the advantages and disadvantages each technological trajectory represents in general terms, as well as the specific problems each approach represents for the balance between private rights and public goods that I have already identified. This chapter therefore sets out a general analytical context for the case studies presented in the next chapter.

Digital rights management, according to its defenders, merely enables copyright holders to finally establish in real economic relations the rights they have always had in law. To this end, DRM first attempts to control access to content, and then aims to either control, or at least monitor, subsequent use – most specifically, control or inhibition of unauthorised copying of accessed material. Although there are two recognisably different trajectories that the development of DRM seems to follow in fulfilling the aim to enhance the control and management of intellectual property in the new digital environment, these are far from being the only options. For instance, systems approaches, which combine surveillance through unique processor identifiers with digital on-line delivery (for a single user) once the identifier has been confirmed as legitimate customer (Weinberg, 2002), represent a trajectory that combines both approaches. Although these two paths may not be mutually exclusive, nor represent the only developmental paths the technology can (and could) follow, they *do* represent simply the key characteristics of the most used and developed current technologies.

The intent of DRM technologies is to *manage* rights to view or access, and subsequently to use or even copy, digitised products or services; it is intended to serve the

| Box 3.1 | Two forms of DRM |

Digital Rights Management	'Hard'	'Soft'
Character	Withholding	Monitoring
Advantages	Owners' control of all use	Flexible enforcement
Problems	'right to read'; fair use; over-enforced rights (i.e. restrictions on legal user behaviour).	Monitoring; Intrusive modes of surveillance; over-enforced rights (i.e. hybrid files).
Threatens	Knowledge commons	Privacy
Example	Dedicated access	Shrink-wrap licences

interests of the producer or 'owners', not the users. This reflects the pervasive perception that the Internet is an essentially unmanageable realm where content users, and the companies who provide them with technologies to reproduce products from original content, are a major challenge to the ability of rights' holders to profit from their products and services. Indeed, the general perception on the side of the content companies is that, as with other information and communications technologies, technical advances continue to outpace the law's ability to regulate the issues they raise. To some extent this is a response to an age that has already faded; although there is still some difficulty regulating and managing the Internet, the 'frontier years' of a wilful absence of regulation have long passed. Nevertheless, supporters of DRM frequently stress the difficulty of governing the Internet to support the use of technical means of rights management. This is to say, content and knowledge industry representatives frequently invoke the dangers of the past (of the Internet's early years) to shape the protections and practices that the more extensive regulatory structure now in place enables them to implement.

Broadly speaking, all DRM technologies are aimed at tracking and controlling the use of content once it has entered the market; once it has been 'sold' by the distributor or 'owner'. As noted in the previous chapter, when there was clear generational degradation between copies, the exhaustion of copyright at first sale represented little real problem (at least as far as rights to reproduction are concerned). Although markets for second-hand goods have always, to some extent, been in tension with the production of new items, the time-limited nature of much content has meant that second-hand resale by first owners has generally (like copying) involved some cost (in the delay of purchase) to prospective purchasers. Indeed, given the physicality of the carrier, the exhaustion of rights has always allowed the legitimate sale of content items once used (hence the large second-hand book market which stretches back to the dawn of printing). Most importantly, and in direct contrast to digitisation, subsequent resale does not increase the number of original-quality items in the market, and thus supply remains in large part within the control of the original producer/supplier.

However, these aspects of the market for content are potentially and severely undermined by digitisation; time sensitive products (with a short 'life') can be copied and enter a 'secondary' market to compete with continuing first sales. Thus, the scarcity that was constructed through the physicality of the carrier alongside the institutionalisation of IPRs is compromised by the possible unfettered use of digital copying. Content goods (including software) can be sold, or passed on, as copies that are the same as the 'originals', while the original purchaser *retains* a copy for their own use. Here the unrivalrousness of knowledge (the fact that two or more can use an idea at the same time without loss of utility) is reasserted, and the rights to control reproduction, which are central to protecting intellectual property, are undermined. This has led many content providers (and other suppliers of digitised goods, such as software) to move toward a licence model of supply, with no final sale, and thus no question of allowing for an exhaustion of rights.

The deployment of DRM technologies will limit and indeed, in many cases, end the secondary markets in information goods: thus, while in the past price discrimination has been to some extent achieved through the maintenance of second-hand markets (allowing those who are happy to wait to use pre-owned information products), once DRM enters the market, originators will themselves be able to control any (desired) price discrimination between different customer groups (Rothchild, 2005: 506). Here, DRM would help constrain arbitrage between different user groups, but equally may involve significant maintenance commitments by suppliers over and beyond previous allocations of resources to the maintenance of control measures. With the proliferation of self-publishing over the Internet and 'open' activities (discussed later) this realm of potential control may shrink, but equally because information and knowledge resources are often not substitutable, the control of important and valuable products (through DRM) is likely to continue to have significant effects.

Therefore, one of the key uses of DRM has been to establish continuing control over copyrighted content/goods and halt the problem of exhaustion of first-sale rights for digital content owners.[1] Or to put it a little differently, the content industries perceive the need to deploy DRM as a key strategy for retaining and protecting the business models that predate the (so-called) information revolution. Digital Rights Management in this sense is not part of the 'digital revolution' but rather a bulwark against its effects. This bulwark takes two main forms: 'hard' control, or 'soft' control. However, although these two ideal types of DRM are clearly discernible, in their usage they are frequently combined and interact to further enhance the potential protection available to rights' holders.

Soft digital rights management

Soft control relies on the behavioural practices and norms inherited from the pre-Internet/pre-digitalisation age: control is post-use, based on punishment for infringement, and the subsequent deterrence of future possible infringers.

Therefore, content owners may litigate where infringement has been detected, and indeed soft DRM allows considerable possibilities for detecting usage. Soft DRM often deploys user registration, post-sale electronic advise of use, utilising Intel's and other suppliers unique processor serial number, for example, and also works with web-combers that can identify non-authorised users. This is further facilitated by the increasing use of broadband and the practice of consumers remaining on-line for long periods of activity. The ability to monitor activity is itself also part of a larger issue regarding the enhanced possibilities for surveillance that ICTs and the Internet engender (see May, 2002: pp. 106–11; Lyon, 2001). This has prompted a number of concerns about privacy and raised questions of the relationship between DRM and consumer privacy laws in Europe and elsewhere.

Although questions about the use of private information by commercial operators have recently become a little more of a mainstream political issue, at present for most Internet and digital product users and consumers these issues are not of any great interest. Users have yet to awaken to the privacy infringement issues that surveillance, and the soft DRM approach, may entail. When they do, protests and resistance may possibly emerge, but at present there is little sign of much awareness of these questions among the general public, although as I will discuss later this is not to say there has been no response at all. However, the required invasion of privacy that soft DRM encompasses has already begun to worry a number of consumer groups, who have argued that such infringement cannot be justified and severely compromises consumer rights (BUEC, 2004; NCC, 2006). Currently for instance, the use of shrink-wrap licences may involve purchasers agreeing to allow intrusive monitoring without fully realising the implications of information gathering activities undertaken by content owners.[2]

Shrink-wrap licences (and their on line equivalents – 'click-wrap') are the most widely-used form of soft DRM. These essentially presume that users have accessed the licence agreement that they are acceding to when they open the wrapping of their software (or for click-wrap, when they click the 'yes' box for agreeing to the vendor's terms and conditions before downloading). While it is certainly possible, therefore, that this represents informed consent to these terms and conditions, given the opacity and technical language of many licence agreements (and their length) it is not clear that users really are aware of what they are accepting when the slit open the packaging or click 'yes'. Indeed, as Siva Vaidhyanathan has pointed out, rather than the final purchase that many consumers presume they have conducted, actually what they have entered into is a 'pay-to-install system that potentially allows for metered usage or even the electronic expiration of the software' (Vaidhyanathan, 2001: p. 178). Thus, despite the formal role of copyright in these transactions, soft DRM supplements this with contract law to reduce or (re)shape the rights that might normally have been regarded as part of any copyright relationship (of which rights of 'fair use' or 'fair-dealing' are the most obvious).

Moreover, the surveillance mechanisms themselves, while possibly not going as far as the actual constraints on use that can be accomplished through hard DRM (see below), can have unwelcome effects on users computers. This became apparent in the dispute over the Sony CD DRM case (discussed in the preface to this volume) and, as Bruce Schneier has pointed out, these forms of DRM are increasingly representing a threat to the private control of owner's machines. The antivirus/anti-spyware software, that many of us use, for instance, failed to detect Sony's intrusion because Sony notified some companies that the software was 'legal' and hence should not be flagged as a problem requiring a response, while other programmes are not equipped to flag rootkits (as these are regarded a legitimate tools). This suggests a conflict of interest for the companies supplying computer security tools; a conflict which was not settled in favour of the user, with the protection software leaving the user not in full control of their computer nor able to rely on its security (Schneier, 2005). Thus, soft DRM is starting to extend its ability to constrain users behaviour beyond merely post-hoc enforcement.

This extension is established by software companies (and other digital service providers) operating a licence system, rather than allowing a final (first) sale to take place. Thus, rights of resale and usage that previously accrued to the new owner of a physical fixation of a copyrighted product are no longer fully transferred (Halbert, 2005: p. 50). Whereas there were certain limited rights that copyright allowed the original owner to retain (linked to unauthorised further copies and issues around plagiarism), other rights were exhausted by the first sale. However, with shrink-wrap licenses even the users relatively limited rights under copyright have been further constrained, because often no final sale is undertaken (although frequently the consumer may be unaware of the actual status of the transaction).

Equally, as well as rescinding or further limiting rights that users might have expected to gain, shrink-wrap and click-wrap licences have been used by software makers to minimise their liability and warranty responsibilities. As Debora Halbert puts it, many of these licences use a notion of purchase of the product 'as is' that is 'much like you would buy a piece of damaged furniture on sale at the outlet mall' (Halbert 2005: p. 52). In other words, despite extensive claims about the power and capacity of software in marketing materials, suppliers offer no guarantees that it will actually work at all, and indeed use the licence agreements to guard themselves against claims for liability by users. However, as many software suppliers are effectively monopolists it is also not clear what actions might be taken by those who wish to resist some of the licence requirements by exercising informed non-consent.

Nevertheless, while soft DRM may potentially enhance surveillance by content owners in their bid to control and limit infringement, by virtue of being post-use, such control is still relatively open to normative debate and mediation. There can be arguments about whether a certain use was legal, or if illegal in a formal sense whether such use might be encompassed within accepted 'fair use' doctrine. Additionally, due to the costs of legal action, small infringers may continue to act with little fear of prosecution, though by contrast (especially as recent actions by the US music industry indicate) some companies and industrial groups may seek to make examples of individual users for deterrent purposes, as will be discussed in the next chapter.

The use of soft DRM may also constrict and abuse the rights of the user. As Corey Field has demonstrated in the realm of music engraving software, the license agreement for many users reserves the rights of the resulting file with the software manufacturers (as regards digital distribution rights). Hence, the use of the engraving software to transcribe a composition by the user (in which their own copyright resides) produces a 'hybrid digital file', which the software manufacturer claims some ownership rights over (Field, 2001: 6, and passim). This use of contract law to (partially) enclose the results of a technologies' use seems unlikely to stand up in court, although few private users will likely wish to risk costly litigation to settle the matter. Perhaps more likely, most users will not notice such constrictions and the software manufacturer will no doubt be unlikely to prosecute infringements which cause little market impact. However, once a piece of music that has been engraved with the software becomes a major generator of income, some fraught litigation is likely to follow.

Although soft DRM raises a number of serious issues, it still allows a relatively significant space for some continued debate and discussion regards the public/private balance; it continues to work with the 'grey area' of copyright at least partly intact. Because it involves the prosecution of infringers, there is always some potential for the justice of any specific case and the relationship between the demands for protection and historic 'fair-use' exceptions to be explored in court. This is not the case under 'hard' DRM technologies, however.

Hard digital rights management

Unlike soft DRM that continues to demonstrate some continuity with previous methods of rights management, hard DRM is a 'technological fix' to the problem of unauthorised copying; it is intended to make unauthorised behaviour impossible, or perhaps more realistically, impossible for all but those with well-developed technological skills. However, recognising the difficulties that technological fixes have encountered in the past (from users with higher-order technological skills), the content industries and their technology suppliers have sought to establish additional legal protection from circumvention of their mechanisms for registering and constraining unauthorised usage. The political pressure that these industries were able to mobilise led to the inclusion of such legal measures in the WIPO Internet Treaties, and led to the robust anti-circumvention elements in both the US Digital Millennium Copyright Act and the parallel EU Copyright Directive.[3]

The constriction of users' behaviour, to ensure that infringement is virtually impossible has been defended on the basis that this technology has finally enabled the sort of rights' control that has always been envisioned by copyright law. The rights of the owner can be fully enacted prior to any litigation against infringers, this is to say the rights holder no longer needs to litigate to gain the rights awarded by law. However, this claim presents a number of problems – not least of all the disappearance of a realm in which issues about fair use could be explored but also the assumption of rights by owners that in the past have not been readily, or actually awarded. Most obviously, the previously unhappy acceptance of fair use within the content industries has been withdrawn by technological fiat.

On the basis of the extent of previously enjoyed rights, it is most likely that the deployment of hard DRM *over*-enforces the legitimate rights of rights' owners and hence disturbs the relatively settled norms which balanced private rights and the public knowledge commons. The development of hard DRM technologies has therefore undermined the zone of accepted infringement, which separated the public and private realms of knowledge and information (the 'grey area'). Technological advances have transformed this zone in the past but have never managed to completely destroy it. The emergence of consumer reproduction technologies that lowered the financial costs (and quality problems) with copying are not new. However, for most of the history of copyright the private copying of rights-protected sources has been either laborious (i.e. direct transcribing) or costly (industry standard reproduction technologies have been beyond the pocket of the individual), and hence there was little opportunity for individuals to infringe content owners' rights in ways that presented a serious challenge to the business models employed by the various content industries concerned.

Given the changes in the technological context, wrought by mass digitisation, hard DRM is generally concerned with ensuring that copies cannot be taken from the 'original' legally purchased copy. This can operate either as part of a licence/access system, or as an embedded control system. In the former, the DRM device acts to link the information held on a content server with the licence arrangements for specific identities held elsewhere. In UK academic libraries, the Athens system of gatekeeping to electronic resources held off-site and controlled by commercial operators is probably the most familiar example of this form of control. Authentication of licence-holding for the specific set of content is under-taken prior to access being obtained, and depending on the system operating this may needed to be re-established only for specific classes of content object, or conversely may need to be established for each separate accessing of specified content files. Once accessed, these files will only allow certain constrained use (perhaps one print command or one download command so the user can capture the content, but not easily re-send it on to non-authorised users).

Increasingly, music CDs contain copy-control DRM which is intended to render making copies technically impossible, although this may not always be that effective as some older players do not recognise the prohibitions encoded in the digitised content. However, as noted in the preface to this volume, the controls themselves can work in ways that may prompt complaints from consumers (and attendant bad publicity for the company involved). More prosaically, the Microsoft Reader for e-books has no print button and only allows the copying to a separate file of a single page at a time, and only allows copies of the text and *not* the formatting (thus giving an inferior result). This method, while allowing some notion of fair use, clearly makes copying an entire book to the medium of the user's choice difficult (Coyle, 2005: pp. 11–5). This returns the users' capabilities back to the realm of the photocopying age, and reserves all the technological advantages of digitisation to the rights' holders rather than significantly expanding the possibilities for users.

Perhaps the most important aspect in the development of hard DRM is that most of the significant and important technological developments that have underpinned the development of the PC all preceded the development and deployment of DRM. Hence, the inclusion of hard DRM in current systems will always be incomplete as they are essentially a post-hoc addition to a technological architecture that is relatively mature (Rosenblatt, Trippe and Mooney, 2002: p. 267). Thus, the key devices on which hard DRM is likely to be deployed most successfully are those devices that are currently still being developed, or which are still going through successive technological revolutions, of which the key examples are e-book readers (still relatively under-developed) and games consoles (that went through a period of development roughly parallel to DRM itself), although 'fair use' issues are perhaps less socially important for computer games than for e-books.

Nevertheless, for some commentators the only hope for DRM to stamp out the problems of piracy effectively is to move to an extreme form of the hard DRM model, which Stuart Haber and his co-authors call 'Draconian DRM' (Haber et al., 2003: p. 230). Here technologies would *only* play DRM-protected content and thus would need to be ubiquitously embedded within the technological realm for any specific industry, from production through to consumption. However, as this presents a backward compatibility issue (albeit in reverse, as normally manufacturers are trying to allow not disallow backwards compatibility), it is only really possible on the introduction of a new format and thus requires considerable industry co-operation and co-ordination, which as 'format wars' in the past have revealed may prove difficult to arrange. This also leads to a deepening of the public content problem raised more generally by DRM (Haber et al., 2003: p. 231). However, given that to a large extent the genie is already out of the bottle with digital content carriers, the draconian DRM strategy may already have passed its sell-by-date.

Digital rights management and the problem of 'fair use'

The increasing use of digital rights management technologies has led to an increased awareness of the constraints that this deployment may put on historic and conventional consumer 'rights' to produce unauthorised copies of copyrighted works. The recognition of 'fair-use' (or 'fair-dealing' in Europe) that had historically been established involved the use of small sections of one work (without payment) in another work, for criticism, for study or for research purposes. Likewise, non-commercial copying for private use was usually regarded as a legitimate extension of the purchase of the original product (for subsequent re-use, for instance). However, as new technologies have produced new opportunities, so issues around private copying have become perceived as increasingly important for the protection of the income streams of content producers.

The advent of digital technologies is not the first time that content industries have faced a technological challenge to their usual business models.[4] The music industry for some years countered home cassette recording with the slogan

'Home Taping is Killing Music', but due to recording quality problems cassettes were never a major threat to legitimate purchases. Likewise, although photocopiers have been widely available for decades they have only recently (with the advent of cheap scanning technologies) become a home-use product, and thus until recently presented little real difficulty for publishers. The first *real* technological challenge to IPRs' private rights regime was the home video recorder.

The marketing and widespread purchase of cheap domestic video recorders in the USA led to the landmark case *Sony Corp. v. Universal Studios* in 1984. Content owners argued that the recording of programmes was an activity that allowed such copies to be distributed without further payment to the rights owners. However, the US Supreme Court settled the matter in favour of 'fair use', and for decades this judgement has had considerable international legal-normative influence on the arguments about the balance between private rights and social use of information products. Because the Court accepted the argument that although copyright infringement was certainly possible, most use would merely be for recording and watching programmes at a more favourable time ('timeshifting'), it concluded that the technology should not be banned or technologically circumscribed as requested by copyright holders (Goldstein, 2003: pp. 119–28; Jeanneret, 2002: 171–2). Subsequently similar definitions of fair use of video recorders were established worldwide, sometimes encapsulated in new laws which recognised certain uses as 'fair' even if involving unauthorised usage, and sometimes reflecting the precedents set by *Sony vs. Universal* in common law. The notion of 'fair-use' remains a significant aspect of IPRs even if is also regarded by many content owners as an infringement on their legitimate interests.

Videotape was still an analogue technology that saw copies quickly degenerate; this difficulty was surmounted for audio copies in the mid-1980s with the development of digital audio tapes (DAT). The recording industries on both sides of the Atlantic attempted first to halt the importation of blank tapes, and when that proved impossible demanded a levy (in favour of copyright holders) on each sale of a blank DAT to cover the projected costs of high-quality home copying (Goldstein, 2003: p. 129). However, the music industry hit upon a much more successful method for stifling the expansion of DAT players and recorders: few record companies licensed their recordings for resale on pre-recorded DATs, and thus, while gaining some specialist support, the technology did not become a mass consumer format.

However, the same cannot be said of the Internet, which due to its multiple uses has swiftly become a mass technology (at least in the US and Europe). Thus, reflecting similar worries about private duplication and circulation of unauthorised copies, the music industry fully supports the continuing development of DRM and indeed has already started to deploy DRM quite widely, although as noted in the preface this has not always been without its immediate problems. However, even the partial success of such a technology will constrain and even undermine the significant rights for subsequent private use of works under copyright that have been established in the period since the judgement in *Sony vs. Universal*. Moreover, recent attempts to constrain this expansion of control have largely failed (such as the recent challenge to such provisions in the US Supreme Court) and the utilisation of DRM continues to expand under full legislative protection (most importantly through the criminalisation of technical circumvention),[5] while other companies continue to produce products that potentially can allow continued 'infringement'.

Of course, industries that develop and manufacture technologies enabling such actions operate in direct tension with intellectual property (content) companies (Avenell and Thompson, 1994). Manufacturers of recordable CD technologies (now fitted as standard to many desktop computers) or those who have made MP3 players widely available, and before them the developers of audio cassette recorders, can only profit due to the disregard of copyright holders' proclaimed rights. The 'parasitic' product violates the commodity relationship, established in the first instance by the intellectual property producer, by allowing the dilution of the constructed scarcity through copying. But the availability of these technologies also indicates to consumers that such behaviour is far from unacceptable: although the small print in adverts makes some reference to not violating copyright, the main (big print) text stresses exactly this use (or strongly implies such use through words like 'ripping', a hacker term for copying, or 'burning' to indicate the making of new CDs). Indeed, as the conversion of music files to MP3s involves compression and change of technical format it is also not entirely clear these are 'copies' as such; this further confuses the issue and does little to help anyone understand whose rights might be most legitimate.

Therefore, against this constant appeal to a 'hacker ethic', it is difficult for copyright holders to present an unchallenged argument about theft and piracy. However, this did not stop the Recording Industry Association of America in 2001 arguing that one solution would be to embed DRM software in all new PCs to ensure that intellectual property could not be infringed, and by doing so limit the capabilities of the hardware on sale to users (Naughton, 2001). This plan, which has been revived periodically, has always come up against the difficulty that hardware manufacturers do not want to market machines that would be less capable than competing products from non-compliant makers. And therefore until the content industries are able to get such technical constrictions forced (legally) upon third-party manufacturers there is little hope of this independent solution replacing DRM. Furthermore, in some cases (of which the Sony minidisc and MP3 players are the most obvious examples) companies are on both sides of the divide, complaining about rights infringements (in their music industry divisions) while also supplying the very technologies that facilitate the practice (from their consumer electronics divisions).

This tension between content suppliers and hardware manufacturers (or corporate divisions) also reveals the dependency on legislation even of DRM's technological strategy to curtail content 'piracy'. Even without some form of explicit (universal) agreement from hardware corporations, there is still a firm requirement for legislative limitations on 'circumvention technologies' (Kim, 2003: 98). Hence, article 11 of the WIPO Copyright Treaty is explicitly concerned with forbidding circumvention tools. Implementing this article has been taken furthest in the US and the EU where not only is the manufacturing of such technologies illegal (under the DMCA and the EU Copyright directive),[6] but so is trafficking in them (which is to say, passing your software 'crack' on to someone else). However, as is seldom noted, the WIPO Copyright Treaty's article 11 should also be read to limit the protection of DRM to that required to mirror rights already available, and thus it does not extend to content not covered by copyright which could potentially be 'protected' by DRM, nor to aspects of usage that would normally be regarded as fair use (Dreier, 2005: p. 398). However, although the DMCA should allow circumvention of technological limitations for reasons of 'fair use', the case of Dmitry Sklyarov suggests that this may not be accorded much weight.

While visiting the US for a conference Sklyarov, a Russian software programmer was arrested for developing a piece of software for Adobe eBook that would allow users to bypass restrictions publishers might have imposed.[7] This raised two issues: firstly, Sklyarov himself argued that his work was intended to demonstrate the weaknesses inherent in the specific DRM technology being used (seeking a defence on the basis of use for research), but also, for those who wished to access eBook-published material using traditional 'fair use' exceptions only a piece of software such as Sklyarov's could have made this possible (on the basis that he was merely allowing the law to work as intended). In the end the case was dropped (not least because Adobe itself asked for the charges to be set aside due to the bad publicity it was generating) and Sklyarov was allowed to return to Russia at the end of 2001, but it suggests that the focus of those enforcing the DMCA is not on maintaining any meaningful public access or usage rights.

It is not merely the question of general public access that is important. Where publishers do not produce material in forms that are readable by visually-impaired people for instance (or by minority language groups), although legislation has previously allowed specialised copying and reproduction (for example in larger print or Braille), DRM may restrict or even halt such practices. Even if they are allowed under legislation, once again the anti-circumvention rules makes the enacting of such allowances difficult, if not impossible (not least as they may halt the development of software such as Sklyarov's). Thus, disadvantaged groups are likely to increasingly lose their rights to access, and become dependent on the goodwill and largesse of commercial operators; their previously held rights have been constrained by the manner in which DRM asserts the rights of 'owners'. These problems, especially for blind people needing technological support, were already significant prior to the development of DRMs (Mann, 1999), but have been made significantly worse with these new technological measures.

Certainly, in the UK the Copyright (Visually Impaired Persons) Act (2002) has removed copyright-related barriers to producing special versions of material for people with various levels of visual impairment. Provided there is no commercially available product that will easily serve the specific needs of a particular visually impaired person, the act allows the production of a version for use (provided a copy of the original 'master copy' has been legitimately purchased). Multiple copies may be made for distribution to user groups by not-for-profit organisations concerned with serving groups of visually impaired persons, within certain limits (not least of all the author's moral rights).

However, what is not clear is the relationship between this act and the growing protection for DRMs in European and UK law, where the bypassing of technological anti-circumvention measures is illegal even in 'fair-use' supporting circumstances. Other groups of specialised users may be similarly impacted, but equally all consumers may find the technical protection measures constrain previously legitimated and recognised rights to 'fair dealing' (or 'fair use') of copyright material. While under UK regulations where DRM constrains or makes impossible a practice that a user might believe should be covered by 'fair use' exemptions, they can issue a notice of complaint to the Secretary of State, who must then decide whether to compel the copyright owner to provide the individual with the means to carry out the activity if it is deemed fair use (Stromdale, 2006: 4). Not only is this a little publicised provision, it would cause enormous work for the Home Office and/or the UK Patent Office if people started to exercise their rights to make such requests in large numbers. It also means that the balance of proof and the costs of obtaining access are placed completely on the user, suggesting an imbalance in the distribution of (supposed) benefits from the deployment of DRM in the UK.

Therefore, as Lee Bygrave and Kamiel Koelman have pointed out:

> Apparently, the copyright-holder's interests gain more weight when a work is to be used in the digital environment. However, the users' right to privacy appears to be mostly overlooked when the scope of copyright and the reach of the copyright-holder in the digital environment are considered. (Bygrave and Koelman, 2000: p. 119)

In other words, the assumption seems to be among the commercial lobby that previous allowances for private copying were based only on the impossibility of controlling such activity, rather than any recognition of the social element of the balance between owners' rights and the interests of the public, as constituted through the policy instrument of copyright. Thus, while the Internet may now allow a use and re-use of digital products that was never really possible under analogue technologies, this *must* be balanced with a recognition of the *increased* powers of surveillance and control that digitisation makes available to owners. A new balance needs to be forged, not one that merely reflects the (frustrated) past desires for control that were dismissed when supply was through analogue technologies.

Finally, as there is at present nothing in the legal protection of DRMs in the US or the EU that requires them to be time-limited, not only do such technologies constrain fair use, they also make no allowance for the end of the copyright period (Rothchild, 2005: 503). This is potentially another further extension of copyright that has gone largely under-recognised even by critics who have been too busy focusing on the current challenges to 'fair use'.

The challenge of digital rights management

Despite its technological sophistication, it is not completely evident that DRM represents a relatively comprehensive technical fix to the problem of piracy of content. A famous paper by employees of Microsoft (although, explicitly noting that the conclusions may not be those of their employer) suggested that the spread of what they refer to as the 'darknet' of illegal content transfers and interactions:

> ... will continue to exist and provide low-cost high-quality service to a large group of consumers. This means that in many markets, the darknet will be a competitor to legal commerce. (Biddle et al., 2002: para 5.2)

The authors of this paper see the emergence of a two-sector world of content distribution: one where those wishing to remain legal interact and purchase content; and a sector where intellectual property norms are essentially absent. In one sense this suggests that even hard DRM is merely a technologically more robust form of soft DRM, rather than an absolute technical suppression of 'unacceptable' behaviour. Thus, norms of consumption will remain a key element for any rights-originated content or software business.

Unfortunately, as I noted in the previous chapter, a number of commentators – perhaps most famously Lawrence Lessig – have argued that DRM and other linked control technologies may allow powerful industries to 'leverage' their control of 'real' markets into a control of 'virtual' markets on the Internet. Control over specific technologies (such as computers or music players) may lay the foundations for an expanded control over the Internet market for linked resources (such as software or music files) (Lessig, 2001: p. 200, and passim). This argument has been subjected to an extensive critique by Michael Strangelove, who argues that not only does Lessig mistakenly believe that DRM can be perfected (as regards its ability to control and/or constrain behaviour), Lessig overstates the power and domination of the major US Internet related corporations (most obviously AmericaOnLine) (Strangelove, 2005: pp. 63–73). Certainly, the success various hackers have had in the last seven or eight years with by-passing or 'cracking' various forms of DRM suggests that DRM does little to constrain behaviour of the ICT-adept user (Chang, 2005: 247–8; Lichtman, 2006), but while these 'cracks' are widely distributed over the Internet, not all users want to use them. The less technologically adept fear that downloading the unlocking device may infect their computer with other unwanted 'malware' (and, indeed, it may well do so), and of course many computer users do not really understand how one might utilise these opportunities in any case.

This problem undermines one solution to the problem of DRMs: the 'right to hack', which, while partly incorporated into the DMCA, is hedged around with many limitations, presumes a level of technical sophistication that is seldom enjoyed by consumers, and thus even if such a right was enshrined in other laws it is difficult to see how it could be enacted (Bechtold, 2004: 371–2). Moreover, the difficulty is that any tool that was commercially available to allow non-adept consumers to disable, or bypass, DRM-derived restrictions would also be able to bypass those restrictions that remained legal and legitimate. Hence, at present at least, the sorts of devices that have been developed to step round previous technical limitations on use (see Avenell and Thompson, 1994), have as yet not been made available in legal and legitimate markets.

Conversely, by antagonising users through (expanded) limitations on the use they can make of digital products, illegal and non-authorised avenues of content distribution will become more, not less, attractive.[8] Likewise, as I will explore in the last two chapters, resistance can also take a legal form, with the endorsement of 'openness'. Another problem is that the availability of DRM to companies selling digitised products will logically involve the introduction of spyware onto users computers, because as John Naughton points out,

> ... the only way of stopping PC users doing what they want ... is to install software on their computers that prevents it. Users don't want that software, so you have to install it surreptitiously. And they will want to remove it, so you must make that difficult too. (Naughton, 2005)

In other words, the trust that should exist in a market between buyer and seller is being undermined at both ends, and rather than helping to solve the problem, if DRM is to work as intended, then it actually further poisons this relationship.

In many ways it is this threat of market control that is likely to engender a more immediate response to the deployment of DRMs than more civil-rights based objections about surveillance, the enjoyment by the public of a 'knowledge commons' or questions about the ability to maintain the 'fair use' provisions of copyright law. Clearly, hard DRM can be used to control markets for content-related goods and thus to fix prices: given that many content goods (books, music performances) are essentially not substitutable by similar goods (wanting the latest book by Zadie Smith, the latest by Peter Carey is hardly an exact substitute; wanting the latest Charlotte Church CD, the most recent release by Joss Stone is not really the same), controlling access to specific goods where these goods are in demand becomes market and price control. Thus, arguments that the enhanced protection of copyright, severely constraining the usage previously expected by consumers, will bring reduced income as consumers stop buying products that do not fulfil their expectations and do not fully allow for this non-interchangablity between content products.[9]

Where secondary sales (into a market for second-hand goods) and unauthorised copies (a tape/CD for a friend) have been halted, the supplier is able to construct a monopoly-like position. Similar to the previous markets for physical carriers of copyright goods, the prohibition on copying allows the originator to control the number of copies of goods that are available for purchase across the whole market, but not merely as regards first sale. Indeed, if such constraints actually halt secondary sales (second-hand sales) then original suppliers, by halting the emergence of a secondary market, further limit the possibilities for purchase enjoyed by prospective users. Where, as we will see in the next chapter, an industry such as the music industry is already remarkably concentrated, the artist-particular sub-monopolies enjoyed by concentrated suppliers can become a vast ologopolisitic system of market control. Thus, while there is a thriving second-hand market in CDs, no such market seems likely to emerge as regards digitally downloaded files because of the technical prohibitions on secondary use of these files. Likewise, in the realm of software, such control continues to underpin the near-monopoly that Microsoft has managed to build in operating systems (even if this has now started to be challenged by free and open source software products).

What this implies is that there is an additional factor underlying the interest of companies in DRM that is not directly linked to its depiction as mechanisms for (re)establishing the legitimate protection of intellectual property rights; DRM also underpins the locking-in of consumers and users into specific technological platforms.[10] Thus, as we will discuss in the next chapter's examination of the market for digitally reproduced music, the lead service provider, *iTunes* has ensured that its files are incompatible with other companies' technology in the sector. In other words, as Microsoft has established, the utilisation of DRM can help raise (further) barriers to entry in markets for digital goods.

However, although market control issues are important, the questions of invasion of privacy and constraints on free speech are also issues that need to be resolved (Akester, 2006). It is certainly possible that DRM tools could be developed that were sensitive to both consumer privacy and also the need to protect the ability to exercise free speech rights, but there is little evidence of any consideration of these issues within the development of DRM to date. Rather, the political economy of DRM has centred on the question of protecting copyright, underpinned by a rhetoric of theft and piracy. In general terms, the danger is that the widespread deployment of DRM has (and will continue to) expand and extend the rights that 'owners' can claim, and more importantly actually execute. The development of ever-more powerful DRM technologies has been prompted by a rhetoric of theft and piracy, linked to the increased capacity of digital technologies to produce perfect copies of digitised resources. However, in many cases, industries that previously have had the rights they have claimed over their products circumscribed by concerns for public-regarding usage have managed to side-step previously socially-developed mechanisms for balancing private rights to reward and public interest in (relatively) free access to knowledge and information.

The challenge of DRM is not a technical challenge, rather it is a political challenge to previously socially-mediated bargains (enshrined in law) between owners and users. There seems also to have seldom been any recognition that the current deployment of DRM has essentially allowed rights owners to introduce perpetual rights through the simple mechanism of not making DRMs recognise a closing date for rights' enforcement. Although John Rothchild, while raising this point, sees it as largely irrelevant due to likely technological changes during the copyright term (rendering much digital material 'unusable') (Rothchild, 2005: 504), this also reflects on behalf of both rights owners and legislators a complete disregard for any public interest in works returning to the public domain. Certainly Rothschild may be correct, but what is more interesting is this indication of the balance of political power and interest as regards legislating for copyright in the digital domain.

Nevertheless, quite apart from any future problems that may be stored up for the public domain through the utilisation of DRM, there are a number of contemporary challenges that have prompted much more widespread interest and alarm. It is to the practicalities of these challenges that I move to in the next chapter, examining two industries that are at the heart of the deployment of DRM and the political reaction this has engendered.

Notes

1. The practical and ethical conflicts around the issue of exhaustion are discussed at some length by Tai (2003).
2. Fuller discussions of the issues raised in the following paragraphs can be found in Halbert (2005: pp. 43–57) and Madison (1998).
3. See discussion in Chapter two.
4. See Lawrence and Timberg (1990) for discussion of both previous technological changes' impact on 'fair use' and also extended discussion of the technological challenges of the 1970s as regards the 'fair use' of copyright content.
5. Although Apple's recent difficulties regarding its *iTunes* DRM in France suggest that these developments are not universal nor uncontested, see next chapter.
6. The European Parliament and Council Directive on 'Harmonisation of Certain Aspects of Copyright and Related Rights in the Information Society'.
7. 'Arrest sparks boycott of US' *Times Higher Education Supplement* 17 August 2001: 12.
8. See Fred von Lohmann's remarks in Fordham IPMELJ (2005: 1045).
9. However, Rothchild does make this distinction, noting that the effects of the introduction and use of DRM in markets where copyright holders have monopolistic control or relatively high levels of oligopolistic control will be very different from more highly competitive markets for information and knowledge related goods and services. The key issue is the interchangability between different monopoly products in any specific content market (Rothchild, 2005: 539ff).
10. See Fred von Lohmann's remarks in Fordham IPMELJ (2005: 1049).

4

Digital rights management: two cases for consideration

Having explored issues around the deployment and use of Digital Rights Management technologies in somewhat general terms, I shall now consider two industries where these new technologies have become increasingly evident. The reasons for choosing the music industry and the software industry are twofold. Firstly, for non-specialists these industries are the sectors where most likely they (you) have already encountered DRM; as a result, these sectors have generated significant debate about the impact of DRM across the spectrum of commentary (from weblogs and casual communication, through articles in the media, to responses from consumers' rights organisations). These sectors will be familiar, and thus the discussion of how the political economy of DRM has played out will be directly relevant to many of your own experiences. Secondly, by taking one content industry, and one facilitative industry, we can examine the broad range of issues that were raised in the previous chapters through a series of practical illustrations.

Examining the music industry continues to set the question of DRM in the historical context of the development of copyright law, in as much as the deployment of DRM has ruptured previously relatively-settled bargains between private rights and public goods in this sector, and thus reveals why some issues around the use of DRM have become politically problematic. Including the software industry allows us to examine issues around the technological facilitation of knowledge and information usage, and by doing so locates the 'problem' of DRM at the centre of discussions about the possibilities and promise of a new 'information age'. Moreover, as Tim O'Reilly has pointed out, the music industry does not really seem to have learnt the lessons that the software industry's initial use of prototypical DRM tools revealed in the 1980s (O'Reilly, 2003). Thus, by examining these two sectors we may also gain some insight into the possible trajectory of the music industry from the strategies and problems encountered in software. And finally, by examining a facilitative sector we can further develop our understanding of the wider issues for an 'information society' represented by the control model that is encapsulated by DRM technologies.

The music industry and digital rights management

In the music industry the deployment of various forms of DRM has been presented as the answer to a set of 'problems' related to the Internet that have been identified by commentators both within, and outside, the 'business'. In many ways these issues echo similar concerns which focused on previous (re)recording technologies, and as such this has led to a certain level of scepticism among consumers and their representatives about this proposed solution to 'piracy'. The invention of each new carrier medium for music (starting with piano rolls and then a succession of other technologies, including vinyl records) has repeatedly contributed to shifts in the distribution of reproduced music, driving some companies out of business and helping others get started. Digitisation is having a similar impact: as before, those companies that have benefited from the previous array of technologies are fighting hard to maintain their position, and the deployment of DRM is seen as crucial to these companies' survival strategy; new companies with different business models have embraced the possibilities of the Internet and digitisation (but have also in some cases, such as *iTunes*, deployed DRM as well) and are challenging the profits and market share of the previously dominant providers.

In the last quarter of the twentieth century, the recorded music industry was patterned by consolidation of the mass market, and now just four 'majors' currently dominate the global market for recorded music: Sony/Universal Music Group, Warner Music Group, Bertelsman Music Group, and EMI.[1] These companies are part of larger entertainment conglomerates whose interests stretch from film production to hardware manufacturing. Most accounts put their collective share of the global market for recorded music at between 75% and 80%, and they remain overwhelmingly dominant in their main markets.[2] Until the 1970s, the industry relied on independent companies in each national market to deliver its product to retailers, but during that decade consolidation and concentration in the distributive sector allowed each major corporation to carve out a segment of this market for itself (cutting out the second level of one-stop distribution companies) (Burnett, 1996: p. 61). Once again, this question of distribution (and the removal of one or more layers of intermediation) is changing industry practices and markets, with digitisation prompting a partial breakdown of the supply system built up since 1980.

It is also important to recognise that the sector's profitability has become more and more based on the creation and exploitation of copyrights, exploitable music products defined and protected by intellectual property laws. Or as Simon Frith put it twenty years ago:

> For the music industry the age of manufacture is now over. Companies (and company profits) are no longer organised around making *things* but depend on the creation of *rights*. (Frith, 1987: 57, emphasis in original).

Companies have been able to exploit these rights, partly in the traditional manner of selling carriers (LPs, CDs, cassettes), but also by exploiting the rights' income that can be gained through public performance, and through music's role in enhancing the value-added of other goods (from advertisements and movies to the new market in mobile phone ring tones). The possibilities of value added spread far to include rights over marketing artists' images on clothing, image rights and other areas where the star-value can be co-joined with other products to enhance overall market price (through brand association). While noteworthy for its unprecedentedly high value, EMI's contract with Robbie Williams ensures the company controls the rights income in all these areas, not merely the direct recording rights, demonstrates the company's recognition that it needed to diversify its income stream from merely being focused on the sale of the (reproduced) music, and is exemplary of the shifting character of music business contracts more generally.

This shift away from a primary concern with the sale of the carrier medium has increasingly, and unsurprisingly, focused the industry's worries on the *infringement* of rights. While digitisation was initially seen as a boon to the industry, it has now become somewhat of a mixed blessing. Digital recordings were originally marketed as a better sound (although still pressed on vinyl): in 1979, Warner Brothers proclaimed Ry Cooder's album *Bop till you drop* a revolutionary new 'clean' sound. Even the initial encoding of digitised musical performances onto CDs did not reveal the full implications of digitisation. However, once digital copying technologies became available to the consumer (rather than merely an expensive professional technology), copy-to-copy quality degradation disappeared from consumer equipment and the industry's previous practical protection against extensive illegal duplication evaporated. This was not unprecedented: the arrival of cassette tapes had lowered the costs (and technological resources needed) to copy legitimate recordings, dispensing with the previous cumbersome reel-to-reel recorders for home use. However, while tape-to-tape copying involved some quality degradation and thus limited its appeal, digitisation has removed this impediment to the full enjoyment of 'infringing' copies.

As there is probably no industry more reliant on copyright than the music industry, much of the popular rhetoric about copyright 'piracy' and 'theft' is related to the copying and reproduction of music. Indeed, this rhetoric has a long history and the music industry is only the latest in a long line of beneficiaries of copyright's monopoly rights to have told a story of piracy (Halbert, 1999). It is this rhetoric of victimhood that the music industry has deployed again and again to justify the legal and technological moves that underpin the deployment of DRM. As the National Consumer Council and others have pointed out, music industry representatives are concerned about the abuse of their copyrights by individuals in their homes, and by organised crime's mass production of counterfeit CDs, but often try to demonise the former by conflating them with the latter. Organised counterfeiters have certainly flooded some markets with CDs, but the real long-term threat to the industry's current way of doing business may be the advent of digital copying at home and a social change in attitude to music consumption; a change that DRMs try to forestall or at least limit in its effects.

The legal protection of DRM, however, also makes explicit that the rights being protected are neither performers' or authors' rights, but rather the rights of industrial 'owners', and therefore while arguments supporting copyright continue to appeal to narratives of individual creativity, the legal regime around DRM is explicitly a response to a threat to large-scale commercial interests. Perhaps in recognition that these protections will still be unlikely to enable them to prosecute the large scale individual trespass on their rights, the industry has also stepped up its (re)inscription of consumption norms; industry representatives focus on the plight of musicians, not companies. The discourse around copyright serves the industry well here, focusing as it does on the individual creator, stressing the rights for such individuals to both benefit from the use of their creations, and to control the way these creations are used.

As Wilfred Dolfsma noted, the difficulty for the industry is that intuitively, many consumers recognise that while the 'intended effects of copyright are to create a flow of income for creative artists in order to encourage creative activities, the real effects are different ... [creating] an environment where record companies and music publishers make large profits' (Dolfsma, 2000: 6). Indeed, as David Nelson reports, with the exception of a few globally-predominant artists, there are few who make money from their royalty payments; Nelson assembles a gallery of relatively famous artists who claim to have *never* had a royalty cheque, although one must assume this means that their royalties have never outstripped the 'advance' paid on signing their recording contract. Nevertheless, most (relatively) successful artists continue to make a living from live performance and thus the exposure that (free) file downloads provide are valuable for expanding the audience for performance (Nelson, 2005: 577–90). Indeed, one recent study reported in the *Financial Times* suggested than the vast majority of artists made more from touring than from royalties, with large stadium-level acts typically making 75% of their income from live performances (Edgecliffe-Johnson, 2006). This may be why the music industry has been able to find relatively few artists to come out publicly against (digital) copyright infringements.

Although unlikely to pass off home-made copies as our own creations (plagiarism), the re-recording of selected tracks onto recordable CDs (or cassettes), or the recording of whole CDs for friends is seldom regarded as immoral or illegal (see also Frith, 1987: 60). Joëlle Farchy and Fabrice Rochelandet surmise that: 'illegal copying in the record industry can also be interpreted as a natural reaction of consumers confronted with a highly concentrated market, in which copyright law essentially protects the monopoly of the major companies' (Farchy and Rochelandet, 2002: p. 182). Thus, it may be the suspicion (or even contempt) of the music industry itself that has lessened the social barriers to copying copyrighted music. Additionally each case of reported sharp practice by record companies that appears in the media (and this is hardly an uncommon occurrence) does little to shore up their reputation as responsible and 'fair' operators.

This mistrust of record companies suggests that one possible future for music is a return to the performance-centred model, alongside sponsorship deals for tours, and the use of linked products (such as tour merchandise) to support the income of musicians alongside direct sales of (own-produced) CDs. This is already happening and has the potential to return music to something similar to the socio-economic model of minstrelsy and patronage that was historically predominant prior to the successful insertion of intermediation services by the recorded music industry in the twentieth century. Moreover, using on-line communities like *Myspace* and other arenas, musicians are starting to both establish direct contact with their fans for promotional and marketing activities, but are also increasingly able to sell their music direct to their fans, bypassing the established music industry completely.

Nevertheless, the music industry has put their hopes for salvation in DRM, and to support this technical fix the industry (alongside the film and software industries) lobbied hard for a new (globalised) legal protection against the circumnavigation of technical protections for copyrighted material.[3] Established in the World Intellectual Property Organisation's multilateral Copyright treaty in 1996, this protection was included as a major element in both the US Digital Millennium Copyright Act (DMCA) 1998, and in the EC Directive on Copyright 2001 (discussed in Chapter two). In the EU and the US it is now illegal not only to use, or develop processes which might circumnavigate DRM software protection, but also to 'traffic' in these processes (to publicise them on the Internet or elsewhere) (Bygrave, 2002). As I have already discussed, there are a number of legal issues that both these laws raise about fair use, not least that each makes it illegal (except in narrowly defined circumstances) to distribute software or other tools for circumnavigation, even if the circumnavigation itself is intended to allow actions and uses covered by 'fair use' exceptions within the legislation. The control of copyrighted material which was to some extent lost after the *Sony vs. Universal Studios* landmark recognition of 'fair use' copying of copyright protected productions, has been potentially regained.

That said, even the music industry recognises that in one sense it is fighting a rearguard action against the successors to *Napster*. While *Napster* ran off a central server and was therefore easily targeted by rights enforcement efforts, the non-centralised file-swapping (peer-to-peer) networks like *Gnutella, Aimster, Kazaa, Grokster, Freenet* and others will be much harder to close down as there is no-one who can be easily held legally responsible (Leyshon, 2003: 18–21), and as many of these products have been developed as open-source software, it is often difficult to ascertain a single 'directing mind' that might be targeted for prosecution. As an alternative record companies have launched a number of legal actions against Internet Service Providers (ISPs) to trace specific bulk infringers. However, peer-to-peer file-transfer is not only slow and time-consuming, for many it is beyond their technical capabilities, and therefore the threat remains more potential than actual. Although the technical-skill threshold is dropping all the time with the spread of broadband, and easier to use copying tools, most consumers want reliable and safe services and have flocked to the legal file download providers that have established themselves since 2003. The market leader *iTunes* (that uses a system of DRM for its services) accounts for an ever-increasing share of music sales, with a clear impact on sales charts (in 2006, the Gnarls Barkley single 'Crazy' became the first single to reach the UK number one spot from download sales alone).

Older generations grew up with the expectation that music would be purchased from retailers, and that the carrier itself had some intrinsic cultural value (the record collector was only the more extreme version of this practice). But, as Paul Brindley notes, the 'qualities which today's older consumers frequently associate with music – the anticipation of buying a record, the tactile nature of handling it for the first time, the sense of ownership as it becomes part of the collection – could well become anathema to music fans of the future' (Brindley, 2000: p. 35). Certainly, music seems to have become much more of a disposable consumption item, and has moved away from more 'artistic' models of long-term commitment to consumption (although such models of aesthetic enjoyment were always partial), leaving the possibility of developing long-term careers based on large communities of committed fans much harder. Although this may further facilitate digitisation and pay-per-play service models of music distribution, it also undermines the socialisation into music *consumption* that the record companies, at least partly, have relied on in the past to maintain their income streams from major stars.

While the 'problem' of illegal downloading is currently not as widespread, nor as easy for the normal consumer as the hyperbole from the industry would have us believe, neither is it completely clear that it *is* a problem. It is not certain that file-downloaders do not buy CDs: one French study suggested that over half of downloaders went on to buy CDs of artists they had sampled over the Internet (study cited in Farchy and Rochelandet, 2002); other research among users has concluded that while file-sharing certainly takes place among social networks, this is part of a communal consumption of music that expands the number of people likely to purchase music CDs by these artists (Jackson et al., 2005). Thus, while there can be little doubt of the potential for digitisation to disrupt the music industry's industrial organisation, it is not self-evident that it will necessarily immediately do so.

Actual studies of consumer behaviour suggest that there are ways in which the previous modes of distribution can be dovetailed with the new consumer practices that are enabled and fostered by the increasingly widespread use of the Internet (and broadband connections).[4] However, this is not how the major record industries see it, and one of the key elements for particular rights' holders to adopt forms of DRM is the perception of the extent of unauthorised copies that are being made of any specific product (Rothchild, 2005: 556). Here, music industry representatives and leaders have always been of the opinion that there are a large number of infringements taking place that are robbing the industry of revenue. However, this is based on an assumption that all infringing copies crowd out non-infringing copies of any specific musical product. Given the increasingly varied choice both of forms of music itself, and also between music products and other lifestyle and leisure activities (such as computer games, surfing the net, and so on), while some music may be listened to and downloaded if it is effectively free, charging for such products might decrease the distribution of such music quite severely. Conversely, the free distribution of music files may itself stimulate more sales among marginal consumers, where having sampled music they might not have bought speculatively, they actually purchase the products they have initially 'stolen'.

Nevertheless, alongside the technical fix of DRM (and the attempt to constrain undesired behaviour among consumers), the music industry has also started to punish infringers. In September 2003, the Recording Industry Association of America settled its case against a twelve year-old female honours student in Manhattan. Recovering $2000 from a child living in subsidised housing did not provoke positive headlines on the front pages of either the New York Post or New York Daily News. Rather, the notion of suing children produced a popular howl of disgust (Paczkowski, 2003). However, it is possible that this finally also alerted parents to the difference between their children watching TV and using a Internet-enabled computer, and by doing so changed the social or home environment that young consumers enjoy when surfing (Hughes, 2005: 735–6). Antagonising your prospective long-term consumer base may not be a viable way to deal with problems in the industry, but equally if the lawsuits have changed the behaviour of young people (through the agency of worried parents) then this could be a positive result for the music industry. Indeed, in the wake of the initiation and publicity around the music industry lawsuits in 2003/2004, US evidence suggests illegal downloads declined and CD sales began to climb again, possibly indicating that previously illegal consumers were being brought back into the fold (Hughes, 2005: 743). However, as with any complex consumer market such single factor causal explanations, while neat, are difficult if not impossible to substantiate.

The varying and ongoing technological and legal strategies adopted by the industry may indicate that the 'majors' will survive this latest set of challenges (McCourt and Burkart, 2003). However, this will involve some clear changes in the way they do business; paradoxically the strongest contender for a new business model has emerged from the software/computer industry rather than from within the industry itself. The *iTunes Music Store* launched by Apple in April 2003 suggests that rather than suing or attacking the audience for music, competition with illegal copies will be more successfully based on the quality and breadth of catalogue offered. Making a back catalogue available that only sells to a relatively small audience is also considerably more viable in the download model than when such a back catalogue has to be manufactured prior to sale (on CDs). Here, the music industry could respond to recent discussions of how the Internet allows the exploitation of the long tail of small quantity sales in any area (perhaps best typified by Amazon's success in selling less well-known and less in-demand, but in-print, books).

Indeed, a study by Piet Bakker (2003) demonstrates the plausibility of this strategy: *iTunes* dispenses with the slow frustrating search for a good file among many offered on illegal services, with only one legal file of a song offered; for parents, *iTunes* allows children to be shielded from pornography, and for all users, the safety of files known to be free of viruses. *iTunes* also includes features such as artists' own play-lists and other (marketing) features absent from illegal systems. The issue of pricing remains, and Bakker concludes that there will always be those who use illegal services. Nevertheless, *iTunes'* sales during its first eighteen months were around 1.5 million downloads a week and increasing, with 25 million songs sold in the first three months (Naughton, 2004), and by the beginning of 2006 Apple was able to report the one billionth download (Johnson, 2006). In April 2004, Sony launched its similarly structured *SonyConnect* exploiting the company's strength in music *and* hardware, demonstrating some confidence in the potential of this new mode of commodity relations (although this has been badly undermined by the publicity around their CD DRM). By 2005, the market was worth around $500milion, and looked to continue its accelerating growth (Brown, 2006). The industry is seeking to re-establish a profitable and extensive core for the its future, and certainly given that the companies are able to earn more per track through *iTunes* than the equivalent from CD sales (Steve Jobs, quoted in Brown, 2006) this may provide some respite from other pressures, provided that the current government-linked investigations on pricing on both sides of the Atlantic do little to force reductions.

Perhaps most interestingly, while *iTunes* and *SonyConnect* have to various degrees retained aspects of DRM, the second placed provider in the market for digital downloads, *eMusic* which specialises in music from independent labels, supplies files for download that are completely free from any DRM-related restrictions. Thus, without deploying any form of restriction on use (and thus allowing files to be potentially freely onward distributed from initial purchases), *eMusic* has established its position as the second largest on-line retailer of downloads, selling around 3.5 million songs a month (EDRI-gram, 2006). There is also an increasing awareness that utilising such services as *Myspace* (following the example of the Arctic Monkeys in the UK) may be a way of securing a fanbase that will then prompt a major record company to sign a band to a more traditional contract. This use of file-sharing and downloading has prompted the establishment of services which allow various forms of downloads for unsigned bands, ranging from free services (often through *Myspace* or similar 'community' portals), to sites that offer sales packages, although not always utilising DRM protection for the files provided to fans.

On one level, it may all be a question of how music is consumed: the market for DVDs has been much less afflicted by home copying (although organised criminal counterfeiting remains a major problem). However, as Fred von Lohmann has pointed out, this is hardly because DVDs cannot be copied in the same way CDs can. Rather, they are a much more complex product, consumed in a different way, and perhaps most importantly through either rentals or purchase can be consumed much more cheaply relative to single music tracks.[5] The cost in time and effort to secure a digital copy of a film far outweighs the cost of consumption (with rental costs for a movie well below the legal download costs for an entire LP worth of songs), and suggests that the music industries' real problem is a question of pricing rather than home based 'piracy'.

One shift in practice that may save the physical-carrier element of the music industry, and which is already starting to happen, is for companies to provide extra value-added material to make a CD a more attractive purchase. Thus, some releases are already coming with extra CDs of remixes, or are released as dual-use discs which in their DVD mode contain videos, unseen interviews and other elements that consumers might regard as adding value to the product. These moves to a more complex product may allow the industry to balance a market for transient music consumption, based on downloads, with a longer-term more traditional market (with some continued attempt to build fan loyalty to specific artists) through the continued sales of CDs. Thus, the deployment of DRM as a 'fix all' solution misunderstands the changes in consumption patterns and the increasingly competitive environment that surrounds the music industry.

If this was the end of the story of DRM in the music industry then all might be relatively uncontroversial; consumers and companies slowly edging towards a practical compromise. However, as users of copy-controlled CDs have started to find, DRM may also halt activities at home that were previously perfectly legitimate; some copy-controlled CDs will not even play on certain players (or in-car systems). This has led consumer organisations in Europe to challenge the music industry's use of copy-control systems (a form of 'hard DRM') and although these case have had a mixed record of success,[6] they have prompted one major player (Sony) to withdraw their system and no longer release CDs with the technology in place (see preface to this volume). Although in September 2003 the French consumer organisation UFC-Que Choisir won a case against EMI, forcing them to remove copy-protected DVDs from the stores, this success has not been repeated in other jurisdictions, nor repeated in France, and if France implements the EUCD the situation may subsequently change.[7] More generally, various courts in Europe have maintained that there is no 'right' to privately copy, rather there are only such allowances as the rights' owner might wish to make. Indeed, as Natalie Helberger (2004) summarises, these recent European cases: 'consumers have no clear legal standing under copyright law'. The deployment of DRM makes this lack of rights more obvious and contentious.

Finally, one of the key problems that has been encountered by purchasers of digital music file playing devices is the lack of interoperability between systems. The DRM and software configurations of the *iTunes/iPod* system are closed, and thus there is no possibility of transferring files between players,[8] while Virgin Digital's MP3 files can only be played on iRiver or Zen MP3 players (or other players that can play DRM-protected Windows Media content). Indeed, for consumer groups the question of interoperability has become a key concern (BEUC, 2004; NCC, 2004), while also being recognised as a competitive issue by the Organisation for Economic Co-operation and Development's Working Party on the Information Economy (OECD, 2005: 95). An attempt by three Scandinavian countries to require Apple to allow *iTunes*-purchased downloads to play on other systems (by downgrading their onboard DRM) has been broadly supported by the UK music industry's trade association (Ibsion and Braithiwaite, 2006). By tying consumers to one set of technological devices through the supply of DRM protected files only playable on these specific players, service providers have been able to constrain competition between platforms. Certainly consumers can choose one or other platforms, but because DRM tools halt the moving of files from one system to another, consumers are effectively locked in to one technology supplier.

This ability to tie customers into a system once they have made the initial commitment is a major boon for the providers of the DRM-enabled device. Not only does this provide them with a relatively captive customer base for upgrades and new devices, but has established market power in the sector for the equipment makers at a cost of control by the record companies (and hence the record companies' support for the Scandinavian action). An operator like *iTunes* can become a gatekeeper to a vast audience, effectively controlling who the content/music company can access. Thus, not only can consumer behaviour and consumption practices be controlled through the DRM tools embedded within the technology, this environment delivers (when interoperability is unavailable) significant market power to a different group of companies than have been in control in the past. In this sense, perhaps the most delicate problem for the music industry in the use of DRM is the shift in market power that it causes, at the cost of the consumer and to the advantage of some, but by no means all, the companies providing goods and services in the music sector. However, this shift in power is perhaps more evident, and troubling for the established companies in the area of software, as there it is taking a different direction which is potentially more beneficial to users than owners.

The software industry and digital rights management

Having examined an important consumer industry, I now turn to a facilitative industry to further highlight issues and problems related to the deployment of DRM. Digital rights management already has been extensively deployed in the realm of software to deal with the problems of unauthorised copying and distribution of software packages, and in this sense was a similar defensive response by an industry to the perceived rights-infringing behaviour of its customers. As I have already noted in Chapter two, the early history of DRM in the software sector was a period of experiments with successive software limitations being 'hacked' and broken by those who wished to retain some flexibility of use, although for many in the (proprietary) software industry such claims were merely a euphemism for the challenge of cracking the software. More recently, this history of attempts to deploy stringent DRM in software has encouraged the further expansion of the FOSS movement. The deployment of DRM in software has prompted not only complaint and critique (as in the music industry) but also long-running *legal* 'resistance' that is considerably more organised than anything the music industry has had to confront, although some direct parallels might be drawn between FOSS and the digital distribution of music files.

Computing itself has a long and often told history, stretching from Charles Babbage to Alan Turing, and onwards into the period of acceleration from the 1970s to the contemporary Internet stage (see, for instance, Naughton, 1999). This history, while important, need not detain us here, rather I will focus on the personal computer (PC) – the increasingly dominant entry technology for the 'Internet generation'. By some accounts, the emergence of the PC from the shadow of large-scale mainframe computing is regarded as the triumph of specific individuals whose day-jobs often involved working for the large scale computing corporations, but whose interest in the potential (and excitement) of computing went far beyond these demands. These men (and they were mostly men) went on to found Apple and Microsoft as well as many other Silicon Valley technological hot-houses.[9] In this history, the Home-brew Computer Club, where Steve Jobs and

Steve Wozniak among others started to push the development of smaller computers, has an emblematic status, as does the Altair 8800, the first readily available, cheap (at $400 in kit form) computer for home use.

As Paul Ceruzzi points out, because early computers were so cumbersome, and used only for highly-specialised mathematical work, there was little reason to expect their use to become more widespread:

> ... three factors contributed to the erroneous picture of the computers future: a mistaken feeling that computers were fragile and unreliable; the institutional biases of those who shaped policy towards computer use in the early days; and an almost universal failure, even among the computer pioneers themselves, to understand the very nature of computing. (Ceruzzi, 1986 [1997]: p. 120)

Thus, it was on the margins, in the computer clubs, with the kit makers, that we find the origins of the (so called) 'information age'. In this narrative, these groups of revolutionaries 'freed' computing from its institutional shackles while the big computer makers, predominantly Digital and IBM, studiously ignored the explosion in interest in building kit computers (Winston, 1998: p. 233), preferring the relatively easy profits garnered from their existing mainframes and big computing. This story presents the information society as partly the result of individual efforts to free computing from the domination of the mainframe, and partly the fulfilling of computing's characteristic destiny as an individualised technological (and facilitative) tool. The individual desire for technological expression, home-usage and play were profound drivers for home building and, therefore the usage and the early development of the PC we know today. Likewise, in the stories and mythology surrounding the later development of free and open source software, the triumph of dedicated individuals (like Richard Stallman or Linus Torvalds) against the power of the powerful major companies (most often the demonised Microsoft) is an oft-repeated motif.

Whereas the government-funded origins of the Internet have been explored at some length,[10] the underlying enabling technology has largely been naturalised or assumed to be unproblematic. Thus, for example, Manuel Castells ruminating on 'Lessons from the History of the Internet' stresses that the Internet had its roots both in the ARPANET, which was funded and developed under the auspices of the US Defence Department, and in the 'grassroots tradition of computer networking' (Castells, 2001: p. 12). However, while Castells goes on to discuss the unlikely combination of (in his words) 'big science, military research and the culture of freedom', this account omits how the PC itself was developed. Without PCs, the Internet would have remained limited to academic institutions and some linked organisations or government departments: it is unlikely that it would have developed into the enabling technology of the information age. Here is not the place to set out a history of the PC, examining the rivalry between Apple and IBM standards, and the accordance of such mass-market producers such as Dell Computer, but the key thing to recall is that without the development of the desktop PC, the software market would not exist as it does today.

The shift away from mainframe computing started with the minicomputer, that while hardly portable or desktop sized, was less cumbersome and site specific than the mainframes. Moreover, minicomputers, with their relative freedom from the overarching dependence on a central provider (for software and for sub-contracted operators) facilitated the emergence of specialised and (relative) independent computer software engineers. It was among this group that the moves to new forms of operating system (most famously UNIX) would take place. This shift away from large mainframe computing gathered pace, as the advantages of smaller computers became clear and started to open up a potential mass market for computer hardware (the desktop PC and later the laptop computer).

These developments finally started to establish a non-technical non-specialist market for software largely driven by IBM's development of the PC, that underpinned the accelerated advance of Microsoft and the dominance of the MS-DOS/Windows-based operating system. Given the growing ease of copying complex computer files, even by technically unsophisticated users, once large companies began to see the profit potential from a mass market in software the need to protect products from unauthorised duplication became a key strand of research and development. Indeed, as the effort to create software has always far outweighed the effort required to copy it this issue arose almost from the beginning of the software *industry*, as separate from the supply of physical machines. As I have already discussed the important elements of the background to the utilisation of DRM in the software industry in a previous chapter, here I will merely summarise its effects before looking at the response that has emerged around the notion of 'openness'.

The key impact that DRM has on users of PCs and other devices is that it constrains their own control over their device, and also may adversely affect the security of the machine itself. The utilisation of DRM systems in software can deny or at least constrain interoperability either by the recognition of 'non-trusted' programmes on the machine, thereby halting the deployment of the DRM-protected software, or where older versions of linked software remain, the DRM-protected software may 'require' owners to update linked (but not necessarily vital) software (BUAC, 2004). Thus, for instance, a DRM-protected printer driver may require the most up-to-date version of Microsoft Explorer to be running (so it can automatically check for updates) while the printer itself does not require Explorer to carry out printing tasks. Thus, the use of on-board surveillance and checking mechanisms (a key element of DRM tools) has the ability to force consumers into additional purchases to get their initial purchases to work as intended, reflecting not *their* needs but the desire of software providers to generate extra business by prompting (or perhaps it would be better to say *forcing*) upgrades. While it is not necessary for DRM to be used in this way, its potential for supporting market control is recognised by suppliers of various types of software and hardware.

This control also allows market segmentation and price discrimination, because DRM can easily halt the emergence of secondary markets for the products that are protected (The Economist, 2003). Although historically copyright has included a 'first-sale' doctrine that has allowed a vibrant second-hand market to emerge alongside the market for new items, in software this is constrained by licence conditions, some sellers' DRM restrictions on the machines that software will run on once it has been initiated (uploaded), and the fast moving market (upgrade, new software) that has made a secondary market unattractive to users. Moreover, increasingly the use of surveillance systems within DRM is starting to allow suppliers to both limit and reveal user activities and practices, which allows software providers to discriminate between various users (for instance through single user and multiple users site licences – a form of soft DRM that is essentially controlled through company audits) and price these different groups access to the product or service differently.[11] While certainly many economists may celebrate this ability to run more accurately-priced parallel markets, for users there is a considerable cost in the realms of privacy and control, costs that are borne not by the companies that benefit from price discrimination but by the subjects of surveillance and limitations on use.

Likewise, as was amply demonstrated by the recent Sony CD case related in the preface to this volume, the initiation of active DRM surveillance systems can violate the security of users' computers when these DRM tools seek to either report back to suppliers, or perhaps more worryingly where they allow the workings of the software to be externally directed over an Internet connection (to change configurations, apply 'patches' and otherwise interfere automatically with users' computers). Furthermore, as Bruce Schneier notes, Microsoft's Internet Explorer, still the dominant Internet browser, does not include easy to use cookie handling, nor a pop-up advert blocker.[12] Schneier argues that this is because:

> Microsoft isn't just selling software to you; it sells Internet advertising as well. It isn't in the company's best interest to offer users features that would adversely affect its business partners. (Schnieier, 2006)

Whatever their motivation, Internet Explorer's DRM means that the software cannot be modified in this area of consumer interest (while being able to offer facile choices about the colour scheme) and continues to interact with companies who may be known to Microsoft but for which the user has had no opportunity to block communications from. And while other browsers are available, Microsoft's continued domination of the 'desktop' still supports the uptake of Internet Explorer.

To add insult to injury, the licence agreements that are activated by uploading software shield the suppliers of software from any liability claims regarding damage (to data) that their products cause. Digital rights management, to use a phrase popular in political studies, seems to allow software companies 'power without responsibility'. Thus, while there is certainly a move to secure product liability for software in the US (see Zollers et al., 2005), up until now this has proved a difficult task; relying on contract law, the industry has been able to shield itself from liability through the terms of the licences that are agreed to (although whether this represents *informed* consent is another matter). However, as technologically adept people find problems that they are unable to fix (due to the limitations put upon the possibility of users re-engineering their software purchases) and because liability for non-performance is so constrained, an increasing number of users have sought a way to sidestep the limits placed on their practices by DRM components of mainstream software products.

The importance of individual software developers to the early history of personal computing has not been diminished by the widespread commercialisation of the development of software. Indeed, the early stages of commercialisation itself prompted the first moves towards an alternative: open source working and the campaign for free software. The widening usage of DRM seems likely to have pushed more users towards this alternative. The non-proprietary model of software development shaped the early, non-commercial period of computer development, with computing source code shared, and development work collaborative and essentially unowned. However, after the US Department of Justice prosecuted IBM for anti-trust violations in the 1970s, software and hardware provision was split, prompting the development of a separate software industry that sought to 'own' code so as to profit from it. As a response to the widening scope of this model of 'ownership', Richard Stallman and others established the Free Software Foundation to support a new (positive and explicit) movement to keep software free from ownership.

Stallman, with some legal advice, then produced what he regards as his 'greatest hack'; the General Public License (GPL) sometimes referred to as 'copyleft'. The GPL permits the user to run, copy or modify the software programme's source code, and if they so wish, to distribute versions of the programme. However, this does not allow them to add rights-related restrictions of their own. Often termed the 'viral clause' of the GPL, the licence compels programmes utilising aspects of GPL licensed software to be fully compatible with the GPL themselves.[13] Crucially, the licence utilises copyright law to ensure it is both included in any derivative works as well as ensuring the GPL itself remains unchanged; to change the licence terms included in the software is to violate the copyright of the software and invite prosecution. While this guarantees that the GPL-protected programmes are never commodified, it has also undermined the development of hybrid free/proprietary software tools.

There are some philosophical differences between Free Software and Open Source, even though both are based on what I term a logic of openness. This has been made much of by the Free Software followers of Richard Stallman, but perhaps reflecting his accusation of pragmatism, is regarded as less important among Open Source developers (often, but not exclusively, building their work on Linus Torvalds popular LINUX operating system). Indeed, Steven Weber's recent discussion of Open Source presents Stallman's political project as an inhibiting factor for Free Software, allowing Open Source to emerge as the dominant strand in non-proprietary software programming (Weber, 2004). Recently the use of the term FOSS has tried to paper over these differences to allow those interested in promoting free software *and* open source software to focus on the key joint endeavour; to establish the logic of openness as the defining practice of the information society. Thus, the key issue here is that both, in their use of the logic of openness, represent a practical (and often also formally articulated) critique of the controlling logic of DRM.

Thus, the ability to 'open up' software that is presented outside DRM-controlled proprietary arrangements allows local users to amend the tools in ways that reflect their own needs (local language versions being one often used modification). It also allows the inspection of the code to check it is doing what it should be doing, and allows groups of open source developers to examine and solve any shortcomings that are revealed through such inspection and usage, again the sort of non-company development behaviour that DRM forbids and constrains.[14] Moreover, such work often allows developers to build reputation and experience that can then be utilised in their paid career. The open source community has developed a clear dual role in software development: providing a source of cheaper non-proprietary tools, while allowing talented developers an opportunity to make their name and profit from better employment opportunities.

The appeal of the open approach is perhaps best exemplified by the success of the Firefox Internet browser. After the dismemberment of Netscape and the 'triumph' of Internet Explorer, the developers of Netscape, although now dispersed across various other computer companies, kept developing their browser and released an open source version (Firefox) that has recently become the main threat to Explorer, gaining market share as more and more people become disenchanted with the Microsoft product (The Economist, 2005). Although Netscape had tried this strategy prior to its collapse, it was only with the establishment of Mozilla that it began to bear fruit. Thus, along with its linked email client (Thunderbird), the open source community project, now under the umbrella of the Mozilla Foundation, has dispensed with DRM to produce a rival product that is becoming a major threat to Microsoft previous dominance of the Internet browser market.

Thus, while the music industry remains concerned to make DRM work for the current dominant players (the 'big four') in the software sector the attempt to establish and maintain control over the use and modification of software tools has engendered a very clear reaction that not only resists this control but has developed a competing model of work. While market control has been consolidating for some time in the music industry (Bishop, 2005), in the software industry, and despite Microsoft's clear dominance of the operating systems market, there remains a much more diversified market for most other software that allows space for such competing approaches to flourish.

Control, criticism and reaction

Having explored two cases where the 'problem' of DRM is manifest, it is I hope relatively clear that DRM is not so much about the protection of intellectual property as we might have originally thought. Firstly, as is often pointed out in critiques of DRM, the rights that have been established under the rubric of copyright, and those that DRM tools seek to consolidate and extend, are not actually absolute rights but rather represent a (now) too often obscured balance between the rights of creators to reward, and the rights of access and use of social information that need to be secured for the wider social good. The idea that copyright exists to further the social good or innovation and expanded creativity, rather than merely the narrower good of rewarding individuals seems to have been lost in the maelstrom around 'piracy' and digitised theft; the public good of access and extensive availability of information and knowledge has been constrained and circumscribed, to become a mere residual of what is left when all other rights owners have exercised their claimed rights.

This is perhaps more of a potential social problem in facilitative sectors rather than entertainment/content sectors, but represents a serious issue for consumers wherever it is encountered, and indeed such has been seen as such by many consumer rights' groups across the world. That said, as should already be evident, the deployment of DRM is certainly not comprehensive and has become widely criticised. At present it is not clear whether DRM will be expanded and extended into new product areas or whether the problems it raises in the end will be too difficult to resolve in lively and competitive markets for intellectual property related products.

Intellectual property is not the whole story; as Diedre Mulligan, John Han and Aaron Burstein predicted in 2003, 'because DRM systems allow their owners to exercise nearly limitless post distribution control over works, DRM using companies may feel compelled to extend traditional revenue streams, to create new ones and to acclimate users to new business models' (Mulligan et al., 2003: 85). Although predicated on the protection of intellectual property, perhaps the more important impact of DRM is to enhance and consolidate the control of the market by product and/or service providing companies, and constrain and forestall consumer practices within the markets for these DRM-protected goods or services. Constraints on inter-operability (that have been achieved through technical ties as well as through DRM related methods) have been used to construct market dominance and high barriers to market entry in a manner that can only be described as anti-competitive. Thus, behind the mask of the rhetoric of continuing to protect the rights of creators and innovators, major market players have sought, and often succeeded in achieving, extended market control.

As I have noted, this has prompted the development in the software sector of a new (or revived) mode of working that is based on an 'openness' rather than on a form of commodifcation (the making of knowledge and information into property). This movement does also have recent parallels in the music industry with the move to non-industry avenues for the distribution of files. Indeed, in the same way that FOSS has begun to remove the large established companies from the supply of software (at least to certain groups of users), in the music industry the use of the Internet has allowed artists to distribute their music without the intermediation of the major record companies, while also building communities of fans who can support their chosen artists not through the (imperfect) relationship of provider and purchaser of fixed music carriers (CDs, MP3 files), but through attendance at concerts and the purchase of directly supplied products. Thus, one might conclude that the major effect of a move to a stronger form of rights protection through the utilisation of DRM has actually prompted a response among users and consumers that has re-examined the mediated relationship of the existing market and found it unsatisfactory. In this sense, DRM has sowed the seeds of its own obsolescence.

Notes

1. Time-Warner's plans to leave the music industry may tempt some form of merger of music divisions with EMI, making the group effectively three, or competition regulators may only accept a sale to outside investors keeping the group at four. Of course, until the recent combination of Sony and Universal, it was the 'big five', which indicates that pressure to consolidate has yet to dissipate.

2. For my extended analysis of the global music industry see May (2005), and see Barfe (2004), Chapple and Garofalo (1977) and Eliot (1990) all of which cover the longer history of the industry very well.

3. It should also be stressed that the influence of the US music industry did not stop there; considerable lobbying pressure was brought to bear over specific aspects of the DMCA before it was finally passed by both Houses of Congress (see, for instance, Imfeld and Ekstrand, 2005).

4. Early indications are this combined model is how the movie industry will seek to roll out downloadable films: a combination of download and physical DVD purchases, although currently due to the much larger files involved, technically the movie industry lags the developments in the music industry (see Taylor, 2006).

5. See Fred von Lohmann's remarks in Fordham IPMELJ (2005: 1047).

6. 'Belgian consumer group will appeal in copy protection case' EDRI-gram 2.11 (2 June 2004), available at *http://www.edri.org/edrigram/number2.11/drm* (13 January 2004).

7. 'French court forbids DVD copy protection' EDRI-gram 3.9, 4 May 2005.

8. The French government discussed an attempt to force some level of interoperability between *iTunes* and other makers' players, although this prompted criticism both from Apple themselves and from the US Commerce Secretary, suggesting that such demands were tantamount to 'state-sponsored piracy' (Geist, 2006). However, at the time of writing these proposals had been watered down to allow copyright holders to set some compatibility restrictions, see 'Apple gets French

iTunes reprieve', BBC News 22 June 2006, available at *http://news.bbc.co.uk/go/pr/fr/-/hi/business/5106400.stm* (27 June 2006).

9. Paul Ceruzzi has provided an excellent account of these pivotal years in the mid-1970s, (see Ceruzzi, 1999).

10. Katie Hafner and Matthew Lyon's account (1998) has become the standard account, which most other popular narratives rely on to a large extent.

11. This is similar to the way that price differentiation has developed for academic journal subscriptions.

12. At the time of writing, Microsoft had just included such tools as a response to user complaints and the increased threat from the open source Firefox.

13. The full text of the GPL is available from the Free Software Foundation at *http://www.gnu.org/licenses/gpl.txt*

14. For the possible international developmental implications of FOSS see May (2006a).

5

Digital rights management, the (over)protection of rights and the expansion of open alternatives

I concluded the previous chapter's examination of the music and software industries by suggesting that the deployment of digital rights management (DRM) has started to have the perverse effect of prompting not a slavish following of the priorities of the industries concerned, but rather a search for (legal and illegal) alternatives to the business models of these industries. The utilisation of DRM does not, as its supporters suggest, merely return the protection of IPRs to what it was in the past, but rather radically extends and strengthens the rights of owners, and as such has provoked a reaction that goes against the apparent direction of these industries' strategic intent.

Whatever the claims about merely protecting the rights of creators and innovators, the target of both the music and the software industries has been their customers' post purchase practices. Indeed, as an executive from Nokia argued during the All Party Parliamentary Internet Groups 2006 enquiry into DRM:

> ... practically everything about the new digital paradigm is a step backwards for the consumer...

> [DRM] means that the provider can now arrange for access to the work to expire, for it not to be transferable to others, to only work with specific devices and many 'permitted acts' from copyright legislation will no longer be possible. (APIG, 2006: para 51)

This suggests that, for consumers, the solution is considerably worse than the problem it has been developed to address.

Deploying DRM as a solution to the 'problem' of counterfeit presumes that all copyright producers (who are not always the same as the owners of intellectual properties) demand as extensive protection of their rights as is possible. However, in many cases (as we have seen in the previous chapter), the actual producers of intellectual assets derive considerable and valued reputational benefits from unauthorised distribution (more people get to see their work and may become consumers of subsequent items) and from other income opportunities that can be enhanced through such initial distribution. It is actually the distributors and mass-marketers that feel more threatened and whose business models are under threat from such activity. Therefore, the deployment of DRM is a political issue that needs to be carefully considered by policy makers, information specialists and consumer organisations, balancing private rights with public benefits, and it is not (as it is sometimes presented) merely a technical problem only requiring better regulation.

It is vital to stress this point: although the 'information age' may have introduced new methods for the dissemination and use of information and knowledge, this does not mean that previous considerations of the manner in which private rights should be *balanced* with public regarding issues of use and access can now be ignored. As Doug Lichtman suggests, reform is certainly *possible*: 'The task now is not to legislate DRM out of existence, but instead to calibrate copyright law such that it harnesses the very real advantages of technological enforcement while at the same time keeping an appropriately wary eye on what might turn out to be overly aggressive uses' (Lichtman, 2006). However, whether this can be achieved in the face of a powerful and well-organised pro-DRM lobby from the content and software industries is, of course, another matter. Thus, despite the presentation of DRMs as being a question of protecting rights, perhaps its more important impact has been on the regulation of technology and the control of markets.

As I have already noted, DRMs can be used to control the use of content by requiring it only be played/viewed on specific technological platforms, and this has led to increased concerns about interoperability by users and their representatives. Although DRM is usually implemented through software, any computer can have a number of DRM systems running concurrently and thus interoperability between different systems of rights' protection may not always be required for PCs to continue to function acceptably. Thus, while interoperability may be an issue for the consumer or user as regards the purchase of additional tools to read/use different suppliers goods, technically much of the difficulty of operation is undertaken by the interaction of software processes unknown to the user. One solution to this issue would be to have regulated and imposed interoperability standards, but such demands are noticeably absent from the relevant legislation, such as the Digital Millennium Copyright Act (DMCA) and the European Union Copyright Directive (EUCD). Likewise, even voluntary codes have been slow to emerge and are seldom accorded much weight in the development of DRM tools.

A single DRM standard therefore is likely to be chimerical due to the other advantages DRM delivers as regards market control.[1] Moreover, a number of recent cases brought in the US against users by DRM-deploying corporations have not been aimed at protecting content, but rather have been focused on the consumers 'hacking' products to use them in a different way; the disturbance has been based on interoperability with other products rather than on the unauthorised duplication and distribution of content. In these cases, the protection for DRMs and the outlawing of circumvention has been utilised by Sony in the games console market, and by Lexmark to try and halt the use of generic printer refill cartridges (with chips embedded in them),[2] and in perhaps the most extraordinary case, a garage door manufacturer tried, and failed, to have the DMCA's limits on circumvention applied to a manufacturer of a generic remote electronic universal garage door opening device (Burk, 2005: 564–567).[3] This demonstrates the temptation to use a mechanism justified on the basis of discussions of legitimated copyright protections as a tool for controlling markets and constraining competition. In the US, courts are becoming a little more aware of the anti-trust, anti-competition questions underlying DRM, however as the limits have not been pushed so far in Europe as yet, the discussion of the problems with DRM remains limited in scope.

The most obvious misunderstanding at the centre of the debates over DRM is whose interests copyright is intended to serve. Too often it has become clear that for many industry-friendly commentators and legal specialists the presumption is that copyright is intended to serve the original creator and/or their nominated (commercial) exploiter. However, historically copyright was developed to serve the *public* interest by establishing certain rights for creators. When these creators' rights conflict with the interests of the public realm or the 'public', however conceived, it is far from evident that the current 'common-sense' that the private rights' holders interests are always paramount (a position that has underpinned the development of DRM) is a fair or plausible interpretation of the legal record and original intent of copyright. Rather, copyright is itself located within a complex set of interacting rights that actually should favour public-regarding interests at important junctures, such as over freedom of expression, or freedom of information, that DRM seeks to deny or obscure (Hoeren, 2003). This complex of rights has been increasingly obscured by the assertion of strong owners' rights.

Certainly, the World Intellectual Property Organisation recognises that there are some clear 'accessibility' issues that are raised by the 'interplay between limitations and exceptions and DRM-protected content', as Rita Hayes, the organisation's deputy director for copyright and related rights, accepted in recent remarks to an OECD event (quoted in New, 2006). Moreover, as Thomas Dreier has pointed out, it is not clear that the EUCD's articles that established DRM's protection would survive a challenge set out in terms of article 10 of the European Convention of Human Rights, based on DRM *over* protecting copyright and its impact on freedom of expression (Dreier, 2005: p. 399). To deal with access issues in an information society where DRM has become widespread, one solution would be to extend some clear rights of access to libraries as public institutions; Teresa Hackett of Electronic Information for Libraries has argued, this could be achieved by providing recognised public libraries with 'clean' copies of copyrighted work with no embedded DRM technology (Gerhardsen, 2006). Thus, in a similar manner to the use of deposit libraries for copyright in the analogue content market, nominated libraries could hold copies of work that were available for public consultation and 'fair use' copying, to be controlled by these libraries as disinterested balancers of competing interests, rather than by copyright holders who are likely to always favour their own interests.

In principle, one also might argue that it is possible that DRM software could be so engineered as to ensure that it was sensitive to exceptions to copyright such as 'fair use' or 'fair dealing', for socially useful and legitimate purposes. However, as Patricia Akester has noted this will always be partial and incomplete, as fair use criteria and precepts 'are difficult to define, differ from country to country and evolve over time' (Akester, 2006: 161). Currently, while the rights' holder interests are protected via technological means under DRM and are thus immediate, the still-legitimate rights of consumers and users are only maintained through the actions of the law, and through the post-hoc challenge to limitations that have already been experienced. While it can be argued that such over-protection will fail in an open market as consumers will seek alternative products and service with less onerous limitations, this takes no account of the lack of replacability between many content products, and also does not allow for network effects, switching costs and other lock-in issues (Bechtold, 2004: 360–363). In other words, any legal recourse will be after the fact, while the technical limitations are effective prior to, and on use, privileging the rights of owners over the public interest in access.

As has been demonstrated by the case studies in the previous chapter, the content and software industries have been compelled by their perceived circumstances to adopt new and innovative business models to cope with shifts in the formal arrangement of productive relations that have been prompted by the (so-called) information revolution. However, while DRM has played some role in these coping strategies, as will have become clear as we explored the political economy of DRM, it is hardly a solution, or comprehensive 'technical fix' for the difficulties encountered by those sectors most interested in deploying DRM technologies. As it turns out, DRM is not really the best answer to changing market circumstances, but this is not to say it will not continue to be used, nor that it does not remain a threat to consumer and public rights of access and use.

The development of DRM is a backward-looking attempt to constrain the market for digital products so it continues to resemble the markets for material goods. This has always been the intent behind intellectual property rights more generally; the attempt to make the market for intellectual products function in a broadly similar manner to the capitalistically organised markets for material goods has a long history (May, 2007). However, this set of assumptions fails to clear three hurdles that the increasing digitisation of products and services has put in the way of the continuation of business-as-usual (Fetscherin, 2003). Firstly, the deployment of DRM fails to really recognise that rather than seeking to halt and constrain (so-called) 'piracy', a project doomed to failure by the very character of the Internet's modes of interaction, rights-oriented suppliers should seek to understand such activity as competitive and adjust their competitive strategies accordingly. Secondly, this suggests that rather than try to make the Internet resemble previous markets (through DRM and other mechanisms) companies should embrace the challenge of a new distribution medium and seek to establish new practices to take advantage of it (which has of course started to happen in some sectors, although only falteringly in the content industries). Finally, these companies need to understand while consumers may accept some (legitimated) limits on use through DRM, this can only succeed where provision is explicitly seen to balance the rights of owners, with the legitimate and well developed rights of consumers.

Indeed, DRM is being implemented by content owners globally and across the Internet, while the limitations on private rights (despite increasing global harmonisation of IPRs through various multilateral agreements) are still largely established in *national* jurisdictions. In this sense, DRM allows content users to side-step nationally established public use laws and practices through technological means to further their own benefits (Loren, 2002: 142). Demands for use outside such rights-control mechanisms currently lack a clear mode of articulation in both national jurisdictions and more generally across the increasingly global reach of the Internet.

The collapse of the norms of social value, both at the global level, and at the national level where owners' rights have been privileged through the legal protection of DRM technologies, has also led to the partial collapse of the social acceptance of the central narratives of justification that has supported IPRs for some centuries. This increasing questioning of the previous norms of consumption has led to what we could term widespread electronic civil disobedience, ranging from the copying and distributing of MP3 files (and now pirated DVD files), to a strike by content providers through the use of open source journals and freely available e-journals. In one sense this could be seen as an unintended 'blowback': by removing the grey area of mediated use and the acceptance of some level of individualised infringement of owners' rights, behaviour that has been seen as legitimised through fair-use has continued, but is now seen as a semi-political blow against a set of private interest that are not regarded as legitimate.

Perhaps the key issue here is the enjoyment of rights and their associated profits by a set of globalised content multinationals, predicated on stories of individual endeavour and creativity. The use of DRM to finally establish robust rights to protect content has prompted a closer examination of whose rights and benefits are being protected. While a story is told about individuals, when users examine who has enacted their rights, they see not artists struggling to survive, not writers prospering from their works, but rather large, faceless and very profitable corporations; rights infringement then becomes a crime without a victim. Thus, the difficulty that DRM has been largely deployed to counteract is actually a problem that cannot be solved through the deployment of technology; users have always been able relatively swift to figure out how to sidestep the major effects of attempts at technological control. Only by offering legal alternatives that allow users and consumers of digital products and services to use them in the manner in which they deem appropriate will the industries concerned be able to start to (re)construct the norms of legitimised consumption that underpin their business models (Jensen, 2003). To repeat: the problem of DRM is not so much a technical issue, as a complex set of social, political and economic issues, and the depiction of it merely as a question of refining and developing software clearly misunderstands the issues in play.

This is because the protection that DRM offers can be both more stringent than previously legislated, and (perhaps more importantly) much more robust than normal, everyday users of content, had ever really understood copyright law to encompass (Litman, 2001: pp. 111–114; 195; also Scott, 2001). The grey area between private rights and public/social use has been eroded, and there has been a very real move to further privilege owners' rights that has now made the previously arcane issues around copyright of much more direct social impact and thus of more interest to consumers of informational products and/or services. Copyright is not a natural right, nor can it be regarded as ahistorical, but rather it is a political artefact of modern capitalism (May and Sell, 2005). As such, while we might be happy to recognise the rights of owners in many circumstances, these interests should never be immune from political or democratic deliberation.

To develop a new politics of intellectual property directly related to the problems that the deployment of DRM raises, we might look for inspiration to another movement that reacted against the degradation of a public realm: environmentalism. James Boyle (1997) notes that the environmental movement was deeply influenced by two powerful perspectives: ecology and welfare economics. It drew from ecology the recognition of complex and unpredictable connections between living things in the real world, and from welfare economics the recognition that markets frequently (and quite normally) fail to fully internalise the costs of property use. Crucially, these ideas were not developed in the mainstream of political discourse but on the margins and then popularised.

A similar position may currently obtain in the nascent global politics of intellectual property, though still, as Boyle once asserted, 'we have no politics of intellectual property in the way that we have a politics of the environment' (Boyle 1997: 89). This is a problem as in 'terms of ideology and rhetorical structure, no less than practical economic effect, intellectual property is the legal form of the information age' (Boyle 1997: 90). Limitation to access through copyright and the use of DRM tools, as well as other high-profile issues centred on access to knowledge-related goods (such as the disputes around patents for AIDS-related pharmaceuticals) represent serious socio-political problems, yet they are still too often treated as arcane non-political legal issues, and separated from each other by claims that the various legal realms collected together under the rubric of intellectual property are too dissimilar for common political issues to be discussed. However, it seems clear to me that there are a number of cross-cutting issues about the social use of information and knowledge related resources, and the difficulties (indeed dangers) of their control by the private sector through a property system. This is especially problematic when, as with DRM, such controls are obscured or hidden from the normal user, until their social deployment is constrained, by which time alternative paths may have already been missed.

Therefore, a similar political effort that produced a change in the politics of natural resources and the environment needs to shift the conception of the knowledge environment to establish a significant role for a broad view of global social utility. The knowledge commons should be established as a global resource, *not* one that should, or needs to be, carved up for individual gain and controlled through DRM devices. In this sense, Boyle suggests the politics of intellectual property is in a similar stage of (under)development as the environmental movement was in the late 1950s or early 1960s. Despite flurries of interest and outrage at specific issues, in 1997 Boyle argued that two things were notably lacking:

> The first is a theoretical framework, a set of analytical tools with which the issues should be analysed. The second is a perception of common interest among apparently disparate groups, a common interest which cuts across traditional oppositions. (Boyle, 1997: 108)

It is here that the frameworks of ecology and welfare economics did the work of constructing a politics of the environment, revealing some disturbing conclusions on which a popular movement could be built.

Although these issues have risen up the political agenda, not least, as I have suggested, driven by the political economy of the deployment of DRM, we remain without a fully articulated and relatively comprehensive politics of intellectual property. This may be partly due to the difference between the two commons; the environment is clearly limited and finite, while the potential knowledge commons are potentially limitless, by virtue of the non-rivalrous of knowledge, and the capacity of knowledge and information to be expanded through human endeavour. However, while potentially limitless, given the time-related value of much knowledge, in the short term it is much more similar to the environmental model than it is in the longer term. However, in the phrase often attributed to John Maynard Keynes, 'in the long run we are all dead', and thus, in the short term the problem of the effective diminution of the (immediate) knowledge commons remains a significant political issue.

Therefore, and allowing for potential differences, in much the same way that the environmental movement in one sense 'invented' the environment, a politics of intellectual property still needs to (re)invent the public domain of knowledge; to reembed individuals in the socialised body of knowledge. As Boyle notes, the:

> ... structure of our property rights discourse tends to undervalue the public domain, by failing to make actors and society as a whole internalise the losses caused by the extension and exercise of intellectual property rights. The fundamental aporia in economic analysis of information issues, the source-blindness of

an 'original author' centred model of property rights, and the political blindness to the importance of the public domain as a whole... all come together to make the public domain disappear, first in concept and then, increasingly, in reality. (Boyle, 1997: 111–112)

By individualising creation, by disembeding it from the social milieu from which all knowledge is drawn, intellectual property rights deny the importance of the public realm. By doing so they reward only a small group of rights holders rather than the carriers of social knowledge, and more importantly ignore the social welfare benefits of those excluded from use, not by ignorance or lack of interest, but by their poverty.

The breakdown or collapse of social norms around copyright on the Internet, which has been prompted by the emerging DRM technologies, needs to be situated in a more general (global) politics of intellectual property: a politics that seeks to reassert the importance of the public side of the bargain at the centre of the legal construction of IPRs; a politics that stresses the need to reassert political rights to knowledge and information at least equally with the currently privileged private property rights. This is not an 'all intellectual property is theft' argument, but *crucially* it is an unwillingness to accept that the only aspect of IPRs worth thinking about are its *private* rights. Echoing the distinction between property rights and political rights, Ruth Okediji argues:

If stronger property rights are justified (or necessary) because welfare gains from increased creativity are jeopardised by the ease with which established rights may be undermined by [content] takers, then stronger countervailing user rights are also required to, at least, maintain welfare benefits for users because new

> technology enables owners to 'lock up' information content ... As copyright is strengthened and expanded to accommodate new technologies, so should the model of public welfare be adjusted to account for how new technology promotes or hinders access and use of copyrighted works. (Okediji, 2001: 181)

For this (re) balancing to have some hope of success, a new politics of the knowledge commons needs to weigh in on the side of the public domain, to balance the well established and powerful interests that have been mobilised, not so much by authors as by the content industries, to protect, advance and expand their commercial rights to profit form the exploitation of content. Looking at the argument this way, any rebalancing will require political action. This reformism should not be limited to formal legal instruments, but rather represents the need to place intellectual property firmly within the political realm of contemporary (global) society, and refuse any claim that these issues are too arcane for political deliberation and engagement.

As Garrett Levin has put it: 'What needs to be created is a politics of expression that educates citizens about the interaction of their rights as consumers, their rights of access to and use of copyright materials, their... rights of free expression, and the need for digital innovation' (Levin, 2005: paragraph 35). He sees signs of such a politics of expression starting to emerge in the form of interest in the Creative Commons license (discussed below) and in increased concerns about the public domain; to this I would add that the emergence of open models following in the footsteps of the free and open source software movement have alerted an increasing number of people to what exactly DRM takes away, by demonstrating very clearly what an alternative looks like. Perhaps more importantly the moves to develop and extend the logic of 'openness' also represent a parallel path to legal reformism.

Openness confronts digital rights management

In the years since James Boyle called for an environmentalism of the net, we can recognise a linked but differently conceived (organic) response in the ever-widening interest and discussion of the logic of openness. Moreover, the advantages of openness are not only related to the development and utilisation of software tools; as many of the Internet's early celebrants fervently hoped the value of 'openness' is also now being (re)asserted as regards the availability of scientific and other information (Mulgan, Steinberg and Salem, 2005). In the realm of biomedical research, the shift to open access publishing of results has been perhaps most pronounced, partly because the already high costs of research are compounded by the high costs of academic journal subscriptions. This reflects access concerns that are central to the *politics* of information in the information society. The crucial argument mobilised by the supporters of open academic publication, such as the Wellcome Trust and many Universities, has been that as most published research is funded by taxpayers (in various ways) there seems little justice in having to pay again to have such information disseminated to the public-sector community served by most specialised scientific journals.

Already, many academics, writers and commentators circulate work in progress over the Internet, and much work that will subsequently appear in normally-published outlets appears either as working papers or as pre-print versions of articles. Although there are few if any mechanisms that allow the quality of work to be independently judged, increasingly the notion of open comments and rankings appearing alongside the original publication are gaining ground as an open quality control device (Mulgan, Steinberg and Salam, 2005: Chapter five). This reputational system has been popularised by eBay and Amazon as a way of assessing both suppliers and products, and has potential to act as a way of establishing reputational value for open knowledge resources. The spread of the weblog as a form of publication is the most publicly visible trend outside the academy of a process that has already seen in the last decade a shift to more and more information available on-line. However, some authors have started to worry that the circulation of work over the Internet might allow unscrupulous users to incorporate this freely accessible work into commercial products and profit from this reproduction; there remains the ever-present possibility of commodification.

The development of the 'creative commons' license, is one response to this concern, where producers of information and/or knowledge want to secure widened access, but want to retain some control over their work. 'Creative commons' licenses, similar to the GPL, allow distributed usage of content, but also, importantly, do not allow its subsequent commodification (or 'enclosure') when used in other contexts. The license is formulated as a menu of options as regards the extent of open access that an author might wish to allow: it allows a selection from a series of increasingly greater 'freedoms' to use, modify and distribute. Championed by Lawrence Lessig and others, this model for content distribution is being actively promoted by a number of groups interested in the public domain and is a key element of the Open Society Institute's information programme in Eastern Europe. By the first quarter of 2004 (less than a year after its launch) nearly half a million pages on the Internet had utilised this license to allow various levels of open access and use (Lessig, 2004: p. 11), and in the subsequent years the number of pages available has expanded greatly. For those who wish to add to the global stock of Internet-accessible information and/or knowledge this model is likely to be increasingly important. Curiously, in some ways this can be seen as a form of 'soft' DRM, although it is deployed to bring about very different effects.

This expansion of the idea of 'openness' is partly a manifestation of the continuing development of ICTs and specifically the growing reach of the Internet and its associated technologies. However, these technical developments, while clearly facilitative of the countervailing move against intellectual property, cannot be seen as its only cause. Rather, and this is explicit in the software community where many of the ideas about openness have been reinvigorated, the appeal of openness is a direct response to the shift to more trenchant protection of intellectual property in the last ten years and the move to extend control through various modes of DRM. The desire by 'owners' to protect their rights through technical means, and through the courts has prompted a reaction against such expansive expressions of owners' rights. Those who seek access to knowledge and information have responded to this expanding commodification by seeking ways (both technical and social) to undermine the rendering of knowledge as a passive and marketable resource (or product).

Therefore, what started as a concern for the protection of creators and innovators rights to reward from their effort, stimulating the development of technical means of protecting these rights via DRM, has in the end prompted a reaction that has examined the initial assumptions more carefully. Although, as with all complex social phenomena there can be little doubt that the move to develop 'openness' is the result of a varied set of social and technological changes, what I have tried to demonstrate in this book is that the reaction to the imposition of DRM has been one of the major contributing factors to this change. Once the deployment of DRM was revealed to be not only about the (quite often) legitimate protection of intellectual property rights, but just as much about market control and anti-competitive practices by large and already dominant companies, those affected by its limitations on use were likely to respond by seeking alternatives.

In this sense, firstly the development of DRM may have done the politics of intellectual property a service by revealing very clearly the real interests of those who promote the narratives of justification that are commonly alluded to when intellectual property is eulogised. Secondly by finally pushing their demands so far and underpinning them with technical means of enaction, the companies that have deployed DRM may have contributed to the development of a socio-political economic model of practice in the information society that will possibly fatally undermine their current business models in the long run. We might say that this reflects what Karl Polanyi once called the 'double movement' (Polanyi, 1944 [1957]). Knowledge and information are developed and created in a social context that is not necessarily dependent on the workings of capitalism, and that reflects much older social mores such as creativity and the desire to discover and communicate. The shift to DRM has been an attempt to further remove knowledge and information from this context and embed them in a system of property rights. This move to socially disembed information has provoked the second part of a 'double movement' that seeks to return knowledge and information to the more socialised milieu, the opposite of a complete marketisation or commodification.[4]

Does this mean the end of DRM? More likely for the present, digital rights management and openness will represent two opposed choices that will increasingly be seen as central to the political economy of the information society. One can choose at various times to adopt openness, and at other times to mobilise property rights and their protection through DRM systems; the most important aspect of the openness reaction prompted by DRM is that has re-emphasised that the control and distribution of information and knowledge is a social and political phenomena that requires choices to be made continually about practice. Certainly more openness *about* the effects on our use of information and knowledge is required, but equally sometimes, and for various reasons, we may be very happy to acquiesce in the control that DRM establishes. The early years of DRM tried to deny us these choices, but in the wake of the accelerating use of open access and open source systems, the deployment of DRM is already becoming better understood and to some extent has already been partly tamed. Digital rights management is likely to remain one among a number of possible solutions to the question of distribution, but it will not, nor should not, be the only answer.

Notes

1. See Alan Cohen's remarks quoted in footnote 196, Fordham IPMELJ (2005: 1058), and Akester (2006: 163–164).
2. Lexmark's claim was finally dismissed by the US Supreme Court in 2005, although it remains instructive as regards industry intent and desires.
3. A number of other cases of how the DMCA has been deployed to constrain fair use, competition and free speech as well as side-stepping laws on computer intrusion in the US, often well

beyond the copyright areas that have been the focus of this book, are laid out in EFF (2006a).

4. In critical political economy this has become a common analytical move; although Polanyi was concerned with the move from feudalism to capitalism, his notion that the more rapacious forms of early capitalism were eventually constrained and regulated (for their own good) by various laws and policies of the state, remains a suggestive notion for understanding the dialectical development of political economy, see Polanyi (1944 [1957]).

References

Akester, P. (2006) 'Digital rights management in the 21st century', *European Intellectual Property Review* 28(3): 159–68.

All Party Parliamentary Internet Group [APIG] (2006) *Digital Rights Management: Report of an Inquiry by the All Party Internet Group*. London: APIG/House of Commons.

Avenell, S. and Thompson, H. (1994) 'Commodity relations and the forces of production: the theft and defence of intellectual property', *Journal of Interdisciplinary Economics* 5(1): 23–35.

Bakker, P. (2003) 'File sharing – fight, ignore or compete', paper presented at the 8th annual CTI conference – Copyright and Software Patents, 4–5 December, Centre for Tele-Information, Technical University of Denmark.

Barfe, L. (2004) *Where Have All the Good Times Gone? The rise and fall of the record industry*. London: Atlantic Books.

Bechtold, S. (2004) 'Digital rights management in the United States and Europe', *American Journal of Comparative Law*, 52(Spring): 323–82.

Biddle, P., England, P., Peinado, M. and Willman, B. (2002) 'The darknet and the future of content distribution'. Available at *http://www.briefhistory.com/footnotes* (accessed 4 December 2002).

Bishop, J. (2005) 'Building international empires of sound: concentrations of power and property in the "global" music market', *Popular Music and Society*, 28(4): 443–71.

Brindley, P. (2000) *New Musical Entrepreneurs*. London: Institute for Public Policy Research.

Brown, J. (2006) 'Track down cheaper ways to buy music', *The Sunday Times* (Money section), 21 May: 10.

Boyle, J. (1997) 'A politics of intellectual property: environmentalism for the net?', *Duke Law Journal*, 47(1): 87–116.

Bureau Européen des Unions de Consommateurs [BUEC] (2004) 'Digital rights management', (BUEC/430/2004). Bruxelles: BUEC.

Burk, D.L. (2005) 'Legal and technical standards in digital rights management technology' (Panel IV: Market Regulation and Innovation), *Fordham Law Review* (symposium issue), 74(2): 537–73.

Burnett, R. (1996) *The Global Jukebox: The International Music Industry*. London: Routledge.

Bygrave, L.A. and Koelman, K.J. (2000) 'Privacy, data protection and copyright: their interaction in the context of electronic copyright management systems' in ed. P.B. Hughenholtz, *Copyright and Electronic Commerce: Legal Aspects of Electronic Copyright Management*. The Hague: Kluwer Law International.

Bygrave, L.A. (2002) 'The technologisation of copyright: implications for privacy and related interests', *European Intellectual Property Review*, 24(2): 51–7.

Castells, M. (2001) *The Internet Galaxy: Reflections on the Internet, Business and Society*. Oxford: Oxford University Press.

Ceruzzi, P. (1986) 'An unforeseen revolution: computers and expectations 1935–1985' in ed. J.J. Corn, *Imagining Tomorrow: History, Technology and the American Future*. Cambridge, MA: MIT Press [reprinted in A.H. Teich (ed.) (1997) *Technology and the Future* (Seventh Edition). New York: St. Martin's Press].

Ceruzzi, P. (1999) 'Inventing personal computing', in eds D. MacKenzie and J. Wajcman, *The social shaping of technology* (second edition). Buckingham: Open University Press.

Chang, Y-L. (2005) 'Does Lessig's criticism of digital rights management target one technology that the information industries desire more than they can actually provide?', *International Review of Law Computers and Technology*, 19(3): 235–52.

Chapple, S. and Garofalo, R. (1977) *Rock 'n' Roll is Here to Pay*. Chicago: Nelson–Hall.

Commission on Intellectual Property Rights [CIPR] (2002) *Integrating Intellectual Property Rights and Development Policy*. London: CIPR/Department of International Development.

Commons, J.R. (1924 [1959]) *Legal Foundation of Capitalism*. Madison: University of Wisconsin Press.

Coyle, K. (2005) 'The technology of rights: digital rights management' in ed. S.S. Kambhammettu, *Digital Rights Management: Concepts and Applications*. Hydrabad: Le Magnus University Press.

Dinwoodie, G. (2002) 'The architecture of the international intellectual property system', *Chicago Kent Law Review*, 77(3): 993–1014.

Dolfsma, W. (2000) 'How will the music industry weather the globalisation storm' *First Monday* 5(5): available at *http://firstmonday.org/issues/issue5_5/dolfsma/index.html* (accessed 3 May 2000).

Drahos, P. and Braithwaite, J. (2002) *Information Feudalism: Who owns the Knowledge economy?* London: Earthscan Publications.

Dreier, T. (2005) 'Contracting out of copyright in the information society: the impact on freedom of expression', in eds J. Griffiths and U. Suthersanen,

Copyright and Free Speech: Comparative and Historical Analyses. Oxford: Oxford University Press.

The Economist (2003) 'They're watching you', *The Economist*, 18 October: 100.

The Economist (2005) 'Firefox swings to the rescue', *The Economist*, 17 December: 74.

EDRI-gram (2006) 'Discussions continue on a development agenda for WIPO', *EDRI-gram* 4(4): available at *http://www.edri.org/edrigram/number4.4* (accessed 14 March 2006).

Edgecliffe-Johnson, A. (2006) 'Demand for gigs leaves promoters upbeat', *Financial Times*, 23 February: 6.

Electronic Frontier Foundation [EFF] (2006a) *Unintended Consequences: Seven Years under the DMCA* [v.4]. San Francisco: Electronic Frontier Foundation.

Electronic Frontier Foundation [EFF] (2006b) *Digital Rights Management: A failure in the developed world, a danger to the developed world.* (Paper for the International Telecommunications Union ITU-R Working Party 6M Report on Content Protection Technologies). London: Electronic Frontier Foundation.

Eliot, M. (1990) *Rockonomics. The Money Behind the Music*. London: Omnibus Press.

Farchy, J. and Rochelandet, F. (2002) 'Copyright protection, appropriability and new cultural behaviour', in ed. R. Towse, *Copyright in the Cultural Industries*. Cheltenham: Edward Elgar.

Fetscherin, M. (2003) 'Evaluating consumer acceptance for protected digital content', in eds E. Becker, W. Buhse, D. Grünnewig and N. Rump, *Digital Rights Management: Technological, Economic, Legal and Political Aspects*. Berlin: Springer Verlag.

Field, C. (2001) 'Copyright co-ownership in cyberspace', *Entertainment and Sports Lawyer*, 19(2–3): 3–8.

Fordham Intellectual Property, Media and Entertainment Law Journal [IPMELJ] (2005) 'Panel II: licensing in the digital age: the future of digital rights management', *Fordham Intellectual Property, Media and Entertainment Law Journal.* 15(4): 1009–86.

Frith, S. (1987) 'Copyright and the music business', *Popular Music.* 7(1): 57–75.

Gakunu, P. (1989) 'Intellectual property: perspective of the developing world', *Georgia Journal of International and Competition Law*, 19(2) (Special Trade Conference issue): 358–65.

Geist, M. (2006) 'Rights and wrongs of the digital age', *BBC News*, 18 April: available at *http://news.bbc.co.uk/go/ pr/fr/-/hi/technology/4918076.stm* (accessed 10 May 2006).

Gerhardsen, T.I.S. (2006) 'Experts discuss balance between digital content access, protection', *Intellectual Property Watch*, 24 February: available at *http://www.ip-watch.org/weblog/wp-trackback.php/229*

Ghosh, R.A. (ed.) (2005) *CODE@ Collaborative Ownership and the Digital Economy.* Cambridge, MA: MIT Press.

Goldstein, P. (2003) *Copyright's Highway: From Gutenberg to the Celestial Jukebox* (Revised edition). Stanford: Stanford University Press.

Haber, S., Horne, B., Pato, J., Sander, T. and Tarjan, R.E. (2003) 'If piracy is the problem, is DRM the answer?' in eds E. Becker, W. Buhse, D. Grünnewig and N. Rump, *Digital Rights Management: Technological, Economic, Legal and Political Aspects.* Berlin: Springer Verlag.

Hafner, K. and Lyon, M. (1998) *Where wizards stay up late: The origins of the internet.* New York: Touchestone.

Halbert, D.J. (1999) *Intellectual Property in the Information Age: The Politics of Expanding Ownership Rights.* Westport, CN: Quorum Books.

Halbert, D.J. (2005) *Resisting Intellectual Property*. London: Routledge.

Hegel, G. (1821 [1967]) *Philosophy of Right*. Oxford: Oxford University Press.

Higgott, R. and Ougaard, M. (2002) 'Introduction: beyond system and society – towards a global polity', in eds M. Ougaard and R. Higgott, *Towards a Global Polity*. London: Routledge.

Helberger, N. (2004) 'Its not a right, silly. The private copying exception in practice', *INDICARE Monitor*, 7 October: available at *http://www.ivir.nl/publications/helberger/it'snotarightsilly.html* (accessed 13 January 2005).

Hoeren, T. (2003) 'Copyright dilemma: access right as a post-modern symbol of copyright deconstruction?' in eds E. Becker, W. Buhse, D. Grünnewig and N. Rump, *Digital Rights Management: Technological, Economic, Legal and Political Aspects*. Berlin: Springer Verlag.

Hughes, J. (2005) 'On the logic of suing one's customers and the dilemma of infringement-based business models', *Cardozo Arts and Entertainment Law Journal*, 22(3): 725–66.

Ibsion, D. and Braithwaite, T. (2006) 'Apple faces a new threat to iTunes music', *Financial Times*, 10 June: 6.

Imfeld, C. and Ekstrand, V.S. (2005) 'The music industry and the legislative development of the Digital Millennium Copyright Act's online service provider provision', *Communications Law and Policy*, 10(3): 291–322.

Jackson, M., Singh, S., Waycott, J. and Beekhuyzen, J. (2005) 'DRMs, fair use and users' experience of sharing music', paper presented at *DRM'05*, Alexandra, VA (7 November).

Jeanneret, C. (2002) 'The Digital Millennium Copyright Act: preserving the traditional copyright balance',

Fordham Intellectual Property, Media and Entertainment Law Journal, 12(1): 157–94.

Jensen, C. (2003) 'The more things change, the more they stay the same: copyright, digital technology, and social norms', *Stanford Law Review*, 56(2): 531–70.

Johnson, B. (2006) 'US opens inquiry into pricing of music downloads', *The Guardian*, 4 March: 19.

Kim, S. (2003) 'The reinforcement of international copyright for the digital age', *Intellectual Property Journal*, 16(1–3): 93–122.

Kumar, N. (2003) 'Intellectual property rights, technology and economic development', *Economic and Political Weekly*, 38(3): 209–25.

Lawrence, J.S. and Timberg, B. (eds) (1990) *Fair Use and Free Inquiry: Copyright Law and the New Media.* Norwood, NJ: Ablex Publishing Corporation.

Lessig, L. (2001) *The Future of Ideas: The fate of the commons in a connected world.* New York: Random House.

Lessig, L. (2004), 'Commentary: the creative commons', *Montana Law Review*, 65(1): 1–13.

Levin, G. (2005) 'Buggy whips and broadcast flags: the need for a new politics of Exeression', *Duke Law and Technology Review*, 24: available at *http://www.law.duke.edu/journals/dltr/articles/2005dltr0024.html* (accessed 21 June 2006).

Leyshon, A. (2003) 'Scary monsters? Software formats, peer-to-peer networks, and the spectre of the gift', *Environment and Planning D: Society and Space*, 21: 1–26.

Lichtman, D. (2006) 'Defusing DRM', *IP Law and Business*, available at *http://law.uchicago.edu/lichtman-drm.html* (accessed 22 February 2006).

Litman, J. (2001) *Digital Copyright*. Amherst: Prometheus Books.

Locke, J. (1690 [1988]) *Two Treatises on Government.* Cambridge: Cambridge University Press.

von Lohman, F. (2005) 'Now the legalese rootkit: Sony/BMG's EULA', *Electronic Frontier Foundation, Deep Links*, available at *http://www.eff.org/deeplinks/ archives/004145.php* (accessed 15 November 2005).

Loren, L.P. (2002) 'Technological protections in copyright law: is more legal protection needed?', *International Review of Law Computers and Technology*, 16(2): 133–48.

Lucchi, N. (2005) 'Intellectual property rights in digital media: a comparative analysis of legal protection, technological measures, and new business models under EU and US law', *Buffalo Law Review*, 53(4): 1111–92.

Lunney, G.S. (2002) 'Fair use and market failure: *Sony* revisited', *Boston University Law Review*, 82(4): 975–1030.

Lyon, D. (2001) *Surveillance Society: Monitoring everyday life.* Buckingham: Open University Press.

McCourt, T. and Burkart, P. (2003) 'When creators, corporations and consumers collide: Napster and the development of on-line music distribution', *Media, Culture and Society*, 25(3): 333–50.

Macmillan, F. (2002) 'Copyright and corporate power', in ed. R. Towse, *Copyright in the Cultural Industries.* Cheltenham: Edward Elgar.

Madison, M.J. (1998) 'Legal-ware: contract and copyright in the digital age', *Fordham Law Review*, 67(3): 1025–143.

Mann, D. (1999) *A Right to Read: The impact of copyright law on visually impaired people.* London: Royal National Institute for the Blind.

Marlin-Bennett, R. (2004) *Knowledge Power: Intellectual Property, Information & Privacy*. Boulder, CO: Lynne Rienner Publishers.

Matthews, D. (2002) *Globalising Intellectual Property Rights: The TRIPs Agreement*. London: Routledge.

May, C. (2000) *A Global Political Economy of Intellectual Property Rights: The new enclosures?* London: Routledge.

May, C. (2002) *The Information Society: A sceptical view*. Cambridge: Polity Press.

May, C. (2004) 'Capacity building and the (re)production of intellectual property rights', *Third World Quarterly*, 25(5): 821–37.

May, C. (2005) 'Concentrated industry, fragmented consumption: the global music industry in the new millennium', in ed. M.I. Franklin, *Resounding International Relations: on music, culture and politics*. New York: Palgrave Macmillan.

May, C. (2006a) 'Escaping TRIPs' trap: the political economy of free and ppen source software in europe', *Political Studies*, 54(1): 123–46.

May, C. (2006b) 'Editor's introduction', in ed. C. May, *Global Corporate Power* (International Political Economy Yearbook: 15). Boulder, CO: Lynne Rienner Publishers.

May, C. (2007) 'The hypocrisy of forgetfulness: The contemporary significance of early innovations in intellectual property', *Review of International Political Economy* 13(1): in press.

May, C. and Sell, S. (2005) *Intellectual Property Rights: A Critical History*. Boulder, CO: Lynne Rienner Publishers.

Merges, R. (2000) 'One hundred years of solicitude: intellectual property law, 1900–2000', *California Law Review*, 88(6): 2187–240.

Mulgan, G., Steinberg, T. and Salem, O. (2005) *Wide Open: open source methods and their future potential.* London: Demos.

Mulligan, D.K., Han, J. and Burstein, A.J. (2003) 'How DRM-based content delivery systems disrupt expectations of "personal use"', paper presented at *DRM'03*, Washington DC (27 October).

National Consumer Council [NCC] (2004) 'Review of EC legal framework for copyright and related rights, response to the European Commission by the National Consumer Council', London: National Consumer Council.

National Consumer Council [NCC] (2006) 'culture media and sport committee inquiry: new media and the creative industries, evidence submitted by the National Consumer Council', London: National Consumer Council.

Naughton, J. (1999) *A Brief History of the Future: The origins of the internet.* London: Weidenfeld and Nicolson.

Naughton, J. (2001) 'The American crocodile that swallowed freedom'. *The Observer* (Business section), 29 April: 6.

Naughton, J. (2004) 'Always time for a change', *The Observer* (Business section), 4 January: 6.

Naughton, J. (2005) 'How Sony became an ugly sister', *The Observer* (Business section), 18 December: 6.

Nelson, D. (2005) 'Free the music: rethinking the role of copyright in an age of digital distribution', *Southern California Law Review*, 78(2): 559–590.

New, W. (2006) 'Top WIPO copyright official promotes DRMs, stresses co-operation', *Intellectual Property Watch*, available at *http://www.ip-watch.org/weblog/wp-trackback.php/211*

North, D.C. (1990) *Institutions, Institutional Change and Economic Performance.* Cambridge: Cambridge University Press.

Okediji, R. (2000) 'Towards an international fair use doctrine'. *Columbia Journal of Transnational Law*. 39: 75–175.

O'Reilly, T. (2003) 'Interview: digital rights management is a non-starter', *Stage4*, available at *http://www.stage4.co.uk/full_story.php?newsID=272* (accessed 22 February 2006).

Organisation for Economic Co-operation and Development [OECD] (2005) 'Digital broadband content: music' working party on the information economy', [DSTI/ICCP/IE(2004)12/FINAL]. Paris: OECD.

Paczkowski, J. (2003) 'RIAA settles PR nightmare for $2000', *SiliconValley.com*, available at *http://siliconvalley.com* (accessed10 September 2003).

Patterson, L.R. (2001) 'Copyright in the new millennium: resolving the conflict between property rights and political rights', *Ohio State Law Journal*, 62(2): 703–32.

Plant, A. (1934) 'The economic theory concerning patents for inventions', *Economica*, 1: 30–51.

Polanyi, K (1944 [1957]) *The Great Transformation. The political and economic origins of our time.* Boston: Beacon Press.

Reichman, J. and Uhlir, P. (2003) 'A contractually reconstructed research commons for scientific data in a highly protectionist intellectual property environment', *Law and Contemporary Problems*, 66(1–2): 315–462.

Rice, D.A. (2002) 'Copyright as talisman: expanding "property" in digital works', *International Review of Law Computers and Technology*, 16(2): 113–32.

Rifkin, J. (2000) *The Age of Access*. New York: Jeremy P. Tarcher.

Rosenblatt, B., Trippe, B. and Mooney, S. (2002) *Digital Rights Management: Business and Technology*. New York: Hungry Minds/M&T Press.

Rothchild, J.A. (2005) 'Economic analysis of technological protection measures', *Oregon Law Review*, 84: 489–561.

Schneier, B. (2005) 'Sony's DRM rootkit: the real story', *Cyrpto-Gram*, [December 15, reprinted from *Wired*, available at *http://www.schneier.com/essay-0.94.html*].

Schneier, B. (2006) 'Who owns your computer?', *Crypto-Gram*, [March 15, reprinted from *Wired*, available at *http://www.wired.com/news/columns/1,70802-0.html*].

Scott, B. (2001) 'Copyright in a frictionless world: towards a rhetoric of responsibility', *First Monday*, 6(9): available at *http://www.firstmonday.org/issues/issue6_9/scott/index.html* (accessed 12 September 2001).

Sell, S. (2003) *Private Power, Public Law: The Globalisation of Intellectual Property Rights*. Cambridge: Cambridge University Press.

Stefik, M. (1999) *The Internet Edge: Social, Technical and Legal Challenges for a Networked World*. Cambridge, MA: MIT Press.

Stewart, T.P. (1993) *The GATT Uruguay Round. A Negotiating History (1986–1992)*. Deventer: Kluwer Law and Taxation Publishers.

Strangelove, M. (2005) *The Empire of Mind: Digital Piracy and the Anti-Capitalist Movement*. Toronto: University of Toronto Press.

Stromdale, C. (2006) 'The problems with DRM', *Entertainment Law Review*, 17(1): 1–6.

Tai, E.T.T. (2003) 'Exhaustion and online delivery of digital works', *European Intellectual Property Journal*, 25(5): 207–11.

Taylor, R. (2006) 'Hollywood copes with the digital age', *BBC News* (26 May), available at *http://news.bbc.co.uk/pr/fr/-/1/hi/programmes/click_online/5019472.stm* (accessed 31 May 2006).

Vaidhyanathan, S. (2001) *Copyrights and Copywrongs: The Rise of Intellectual Property and How it Threatens Creativity*. New York: New York University Press.

Waldron, J. (1993) 'From authors to copiers: individual rights and social values in intellectual property', *Chicago-Kent Law Review*, 68: 841–87.

Weber, S. (2004) *The Success of Open Source*. Cambridge, MA: Harvard University Press.

Weinberg, J. (2002) 'Hardware-based ID, rights management and trusted systems', in eds N. Elkin-Koren and N.W. Netanel, *The Commodification of Information*. The Hague: Kluwer Law International.

Wentworth, D. (2005) 'A declaration of technology independence', *Corante*, available at *http://www.copyfight .corante.com/archives/2005/03/21/a_declaration_of_ technology_independence* (accessed 22 February 2006).

Winston, B. (1998) *Media Technology and Society. A History: From the Telegraph to the Internet*. London: Routledge.

Yu, P. (2004) 'The escalating copyright wars', *Hofstra Law Review*, 32(Spring): 907–51.

Zollers, F.E., McMullin, A., Hurd. S.N. and Shears, P. (2005) 'No more soft landings for software: liability for defects in an industry that has come of age', *Santa Clara Computer and High Technology Law Journal*, 21(4): 745–82.

Index